Endorsements

"Kaye Miller is as captivating in her storytelling as she is in her writing. Having heard her relay many of these stories in person, I found myself hearing her voice as I read. Her love for the Lord and His mission and her desire to lead others into a missional lifestyle are evident in each of these heartwarming stories of faith and compassionate love for all people. *Called to Love* is a must-read for anyone seeking to live out the Great Commission each day."
—**Wanda Lee**, executive director/treasurer, Woman's Missionary Union (WMU); author, *Live the Call*

"*Called to Love* is a compelling account of what love can do in you and through you. I commend this book to you. Kaye is biblically straight, practical in focus, and warmhearted in her approach. Read and see how seeing through love eyes can change your life."
—**Dr. Frank S. Page**, pastor and former president of the Southern Baptist Convention; author, *The Nehemiah Factor*

"More than a memoir, this book shows us what love looks like in the nitty-gritty of life. All you have to do is make yourself available to the Lord and He will show you how to love, who to love, and where to start. Prepare to be challenged, encouraged, and pulled out of your comfort zone as you read about Kaye Miller's own journey into the heart of God's love. *Called to Love* will help all of us reach beyond ourselves and make a positive difference through the simple act of loving others in Jesus's name."
—**Dr. Ray Pritchard**, president, Keep Believing Ministries; author, *An Anchor for the Soul, The Healing Power of Forgiveness*, and *Why Did This Happen to Me?*

"*Called to Love* is a wonderful walk through the missions landscape that was and is Kaye Miller's passion. With delightful clarity, she brings her experiences to us, and applies homespun and biblical principles in a way that compels us to look within ourselves at how we cross cultural boundaries, whether 'over there' or right here at home. This book needs to be read by those preparing to serve and those who want to better understand those servers they support.
—**Brent Lindquist**, PhD, president, Link Care Center

"Biblical...personal...practical...passionate...relevant. These are just a few descriptions of Kaye Miller's timely writing of *Called to Love*. You will laugh and you will cry, but most of all, you will be challenged by Kaye's real-life missionary experiences. This is a must-read for every pastor, staff member, and missions leader who wants to better understand the urgency of missional living in today's turbulent world."
—**Dr. Gary Hollingsworth**, senior pastor, Immanuel Baptist Church

"*Called to Love* reminds us of God's deep love for us and for the nations. Through Christ-honoring testimonies and biblical reflections, Miller paints portraits of the call to respond to God's love and manifest it to others, whether at home or abroad. You will be drawn to a deeper dependence on God's love and more faithful expression of it at home and around the world."
—**M. David Sills**, DMiss, PhD, professor of missions and cultural anthropology, Southern Baptist Theological Seminary; author, *The Missionary Call*

"*Called to Love* reveals the depth of love and compassion Kaye Miller has for people who need to know Jesus, need to be comforted by Jesus, and who need to go where the love of Jesus is sending them. It affirms deeply her role as a leader and motivator of women and girls as missionaries where they are, wherever God sends them, and to whom God sends them."
—**Rev. George Bullard**, DMin, author, *Pursuing the Full Kingdom Potential of Your Congregation* and *Every Congregation Needs a Little Conflict*

"Kaye Miller recognizes that Jesus loves people. She drives her points home through quotations from a wide variety of authors, illustrations of vibrant Christians, and especially moving stories from Thailand where she grew up. She challenges us to bring her teaching home through searching, practical questions at the end of each chapter.

"The power of her presentation comes from her personal experiences as a child, college student, mother, wife, and church member. She shows us from her own experience what it means to truly love people with Jesus's love."

—**Jack Voelkel**, professor in the Biblical Seminary of Colombia; author of two columns ("Ask Jack" and "Great Cloud of Witnesses") at www.urbana.org.

"Kaye Miller's first love for the Lord and all His people is magnetic in *Called to Love*. Powerful Scripture, poignant illustrations, and pertinent quotations are woven into her personal story of observing, answering, and living God's love call. This irrefutable case for the priority of dynamic love in the life of each Christ follower challenges me to respond with Christlike compassion."

—**Janet Hoffman**, former national WMU president (2000–2005)

"I have known Kaye Miller for two decades as her pastor and friend. I am so pleased that her passion for missions has led her to write this book. Reaching the nations and ministering to all people is simply in Kaye's DNA! The stories in this book are moving. The challenge is clear. May the Lord use Kaye and *Called to Love* to inspire many to live authentically as Christ followers."

—**Rex M. Horne, Jr.**, president, Ouachita Baptist University

CALLED TO

Love

Stories *of* Compassion, Faith, *and* God's Amazing Grace

KAYE MILLER

NEW HOPE
PUBLISHERS
Birmingham Alabama

New Hope® Publishers
P. O. Box 12065
Birmingham, AL 35202-2065
www.newhopepublishers.com
New Hope Publishers is a division of WMU®.

Library of Congress Cataloging-in-Publication Data
Miller, Kaye, 1953-
  Called to love : stories of compassion, faith, and God's amazing grace / Kaye Miller.
    p. cm.
  Includes bibliographical references.
  ISBN 978-1-59669-235-0 (sc)
  1. Christian life. 2. Spiritual life. 3. Love--Religious aspects--Christianity. 4. Missions--Thailand. I. Title.
  BV4501.3.M545 2008
  242--dc22
                                          2008039058

Unless otherwise noted, Scripture quotations are taken from the Holman Christian Standard Bible © copyright 2000 by Holman Bible Publishers. Used by permission.
    Scripture quotations marked NIV are taken from the HOLY BIBLE, NEW INTERNATIONAL VERSION®. NIV®. Copyright©1973, 1978, 1984 by International Bible Society. Used by permission of Zondervan. All rights reserved.
    Scripture quotations marked KJV are taken from The Holy Bible, King James Version.

ISBN-10: 1-59669-235-9
ISBN-13: 978-1-59669-235-0
N094132 • 0409 • 4M1

꧁

Dedication

This book is dedicated to my parents—Jo and Harlan Willis—
missionaries to Bangkla, Thailand. Thank you for living a
missional lifestyle for me to see and learn from. Thank you for
showing me that I need to love with all my heart, soul, mind,
and strength.

꧁

Contents

Acknowledgments

God challenges me to love as *He* loves. As I look back over my life as a missionary kid (MK), a wife and mother, a nurse, and a Woman's Missionary Union® (WMU®) member, I see how His hand has woven all my life experiences to help me love as He loves—through all my senses.

Without my family members, both immediate and extended, this book could not have been written. I am grateful to godly parents, Jo and Harlan Willis, who raised me up to know what it is to live a missionary lifestyle from an early age. To my sisters, Robin and Carol, and brother, Paul, who gave much material to write about, I am grateful for their influence in my life.

I am thankful for my incredible husband, Mark, who challenges me and encourages me daily to be all that the Lord desires, and who has loved me through it all. Jenny and Jason, Julie and Christian, Rachael, and John Mark are wonderful children whom I love with all my heart and who keep me on my toes! This next generation is certainly brighter because of them, and, of course, my two incredible grandchildren, who I pray will continue to grow to love as the Lord loves.

I am so thankful for Dr. Andy Wood, without whom this book would not be complete. His love for the Lord shines brightly, and his many gifts are greatly acknowledged. I am grateful for the way Andy has challenged me along the way to think and rethink this book's contents.

Woman's Missionary Union has played an important part in my learning to love the Lord with all that I am. WMU not only taught me, but has enabled me to teach others about loving Him where we live, in the US and around the world, and for that I am so thankful.

Living a missional lifestyle is what has motivated this book so that new generations of believers will want to love the Lord with all they are—heart, soul, mind, and strength—and will love as *He* loves.

Introduction

When a package arrived, this was always special to us. We literally lived halfway around the world. Everybody would get excited when a family member or a Woman's Missionary Union group sent us boxes filled with supplies and goodies. Sometimes we'd open them up to find foods from America we couldn't obtain in Thailand. All the missionaries appreciated receiving supplies to be used for ministry activities, such as Vacation Bible School (VBS). Mother loved getting canned goods and pecans for baking. We kids looked forward to the treats—toys, real Hershey bars, M&M's, and Dubble Bubble gum.

Being children of the 1960s, we once received a package with a happy-looking sticker plastered on the outside. Next to a bright yellow smiley face was a cheerful message that said, "Smile! Jesus loves you."

A pleasant thought. The theme of this book, however, is that the love of Jesus calls us to much more than a smile. He calls us to take the love that puts a smile on our own faces and real joy in our hearts and to share that love with the world. Relentlessly, redemptively, faithfully, and patiently, we are to freely give what we have freely received.

The profound, unconditional love of God calls us to love in similarly extraordinary ways:

- Believe! Jesus loves you.
- Worship! Jesus loves you.
- Search! Jesus loves you.
- Listen! Jesus loves you.
- Touch! Jesus loves you.
- Think! Jesus loves you.
- Feel! Jesus loves you.
- Call out to your neighbor! Jesus loves you.
- Heal the broken! Jesus loves you.

- Proclaim to the nations! Jesus loves you.
- Give lavishly! Jesus loves you.
- Shatter the darkness! Jesus loves you.

Love calls, and perfect love calls deeply. It begins with a response to God's overflowing love. There's no way to love your most trusted intimates, much less your enemies, unless first you learn to give and receive what Jesus referred to as "first love" in Revelation 2. That's what Part 1 of this book is about.

Part 2 is about perception. It's hard to love someone we don't understand. It's impossible to love others as Jesus loves them until we learn to see, hear, touch, think, and feel through His perspective. The good news, as chapters 3–7 describe, is that He has actually made His perspective available to any and all of us who care to seek it. You *can* see with His eyes and perceive with His perspective. And when you and I take the time to do so, love is more reachable, more understandable.

But what does love actually *do*? What does Jesus call us to as disciples and servants? For answers to that question, we look into the ministry of Jesus Himself in Part 3. If we are to be the hands, the feet, the heart of Jesus to the world, I can think of no better place to start than imitating Him, as little children. Jesus uniquely expressed love, not just to His generation, but to all generations to come, as He called out ordinary, untrained men and women to become what they *could* be in Him. He fulfilled His own anointing to heal the brokenhearted and every manner of disease; then He sends us forth to heal in His name. He loved His generation enough to proclaim the good news of the kingdom of God. Is it any wonder that the church for all time is built on a similar platform we call the Great Commission? He gave to anyone who asked of Him, and gave more to a world that rejected Him, because He understood that the nature of love is to give. And He overcame the forces of sin and hopelessness by confronting their source and declaring a new day of good news had come.

We are who we are because of the people who love us—particularly the ones who show us God's love. In this book you will be introduced to the people who have loved me enough to teach me and challenge me, heal me, laugh and cry with me, serve and serve with me, and give me a lifetime of reasons to say thank you. From the football star I married

- to a Thai leper I taught to read;
- to a Canadian woman who trusted Christ in a doughnut shop;
- to an Arkansas dentist who, even after death, continues to testify to me of love;
- to the many people whose names I can't even tell you because of security risks.

This is their story and the story of countless others.

This is *your* story too. Without your participation, your availability, and your engagement in the Plan of the Ages, this book is meaningless. If this is nothing more than an assigned emphasis book or a stack of stories, you and I have already missed the most important character in the book—*you*. So I invite you to join me on a lifelong journey, where the stakes are literally eternal. For us. And for the world that comes to our doorsteps every day.

- His love is calling.
- He awaits our response.

Part 1

Offer It Up

"Freely you have received, freely give"
Matthew 10:8 NIV.

*Those words of Jesus from Matthew's Gospel remind us
that before we can offer genuine love to others, we must
first receive and give it to Him. In this section, we'll look at
cultivating an overflowing love that flows freely between us
and the Lord. This love is built on God's lavish grace, and is
experienced in terms of what Jesus calls "first love."*

Chapter 1

Love Overflowing

My daddy loved him.

That is the only way to describe the transformation I witnessed in the life of a social and medical outcast. It's the only explanation for the change I experienced in my own life as well. Someone greater—much greater than my father—had poured His unconditional love into Daddy's trusting heart. And on this day, that love of Jesus overflowed from my father to a leper. Past the foul odor of his wounds and bandages. Past the fear and loathing that accompanied this man and his disease. Past the culture of darkness that held our leper friend in spiritual blindness for nearly all his life. Jesus loved Daddy with enough love for both of them. I saw it. And that same love, on that same day, changed my life too.

This is a journey that began near a paraffin bath, in a leper clinic in Southeast Asia. It's a journey of grace and joy and peace. It's about the discovery of a life calling—how in a sense we're all unique and, in another sense, you and I share the same life purpose. Mostly it's about how I discovered that Jesus Christ really loves me, and can love the world *through* me. You too. Somewhere in your realm of influence is someone who will only discover that God loves him or her when His love overflows from you. This journey is about a "call."

I can't think of a time when I didn't hear my parents talk about "the call." As medical missionaries, they not only talked it—they lived it. And because of what I saw in them, I experienced the same love, grace, and life calling as they did. When I was five years old, my parents were appointed as missionaries. Dad, a surgeon, knew God called him to medical missions while he was still in medical school. The same goes for Mom, a nurse who heard the Lord call her to medical missions early in her life. When they married, the Lord called them both to be medical missionaries to a small Buddhist village in Thailand called Bangkla. They took three small girls there (my brother was born later) to be the light of Jesus Christ in a dark, unnoticed, quaint village in rural Asia. He called them to be His hands, His feet, His heart there. But the Lord didn't call only our parents; He called us as a family. Even as a young child, I knew that I was supposed to be there in my new home and I learned what it means to love as God loves by watching my parents' model.

With the monies given through our missions organization, my parents led out in building a 25-bed hospital and a leper clinic. Just as in Bible days, many Thai people had leprosy. Have you ever seen anyone with that disease? It mainly affects the skin, the peripheral nerves, and other structures. Gary Thomas, in his book *The Beautiful Fight*, gives this gripping description of what lepers encounter:

Leprosy is an insidious malady in which bacteria seek refuge in the nerves and then proceed to destroy them, one by one. Since the bacteria prefer the cooler parts of the body, toes, fingers, eyes, earlobes, and noses are most vulnerable. When your nerves lose all sensitivity, you become your own worst enemy, not realizing the damage you're causing to your own body. You could literally rub your eyes blind.

Because they lose feeling in their nerve endings, leprosy patients often hurt their hands and feet or burn themselves. This is a disfiguring disease, and as in Bible days, it results in the sufferer being an outcast from society and even being rejected by family.

Jesus modeled for us with His own life what it meant to have compassion for those with this type of disease. Not only did He heal lepers, but in doing so He physically touched them (Matthew 8:3). My parents were able to help build a sanctuary for these outcasts in Thailand. My dad would operate on them, and often would release the tendons in their maimed and disfigured hands so that they could use their hands to make a living by carving objects out of teakwood and selling them. My sisters and I loved going with Dad on his rounds to visit patients.

My sisters and I would go see the leprosy patients on our own.

In the evenings, we would go with Dad as he checked on the patients there in the leper clinic. We had many really good friends there, and we also especially enjoyed something known as the paraffin bath.

A paraffin bath is a huge vat, about knee-deep, and slightly smaller than a bathtub. Filled with melted wax, Dad used it to provide heat therapy to leprosy and arthritis patients. As the patients would dip their hands or feet into the wax, the heat would soften the joints and extremities and provide new flexibility. The wax would cool quickly, and the patients would dip again and again, sealing in the heat and bringing comfort and relief from the pain.

Sometimes—when our parents weren't around—my sisters and I would go see the leprosy patients on our own and do a little dipping of our own in the paraffin bath. It was one of the many fun things we experienced as MKs (missionary kids). We would enjoy the heat. We would also make pretend casts and shapes of our fingertips and hands with the rapidly cooling wax.

One day I was with my dad when he made rounds at the clinic. One of my friends with leprosy sat beside me, carving a wooden elephant from teakwood. Dr. Willis, my dad, had operated on my friend's hands to give him better range of motion. On this day, Dad had come by to see how the patient was doing and to look at the surgery site. They sat down on the floor facing each other, and my dad slowly unwound the bloody, foul-smelling bandages. Bloody, maimed, and ugly hands seemed to jump out at me. My dad firmly and deliberately took the young man's hands into his own, and gently began to check them. I listened as Daddy, with tears running down his face, held this man's hands, and told him about the Great Physician who could heal him where no one else could—in his heart. I listened as Dad told him that he would be made whole one day, and would live with Jesus forever, if he made Him Lord and Savior of his life. With tears streaming down all of our faces—all of us realizing God's great love and forgiveness—the leper accepted Christ.

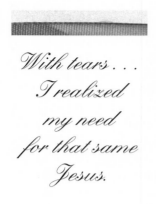

With tears . . . I realized my need for that same Jesus.

I did too.

With tears running down my face, I realized my need for that same Jesus—our Lord and Savior—as my personal Savior. I experienced His overflowing love for the first time ever on the day I asked Him into my heart. Surrounded by medical outcasts in a leper's building beside the hospital in Bangkla, Thailand, I realized that God not only loved my ailing friends as they were, He loved me too—as I was—and am. I realized His love was enough to overcome anything that might come—even if it were leprosy. Even as a young child, I had a life-changing encounter with the grace, calling, and overflowing love of Jesus.

Overflowing Love: Three Perspectives

If you have that personal, intimate relationship with Jesus Christ, you, too, have started on a journey with Him that began the moment you said yes to His invitation. If you have not accepted His invitation, I encourage you to accept this free gift from God now. This journey is a call to receive God's love and to freely give it to others. God's call is a journey that moves us along the path of learning to do what is right in everyday situations to loving a life of serving Him—of making a difference in the lives of others. Challenges, questions, and roadblocks are parts of that journey; but with Jesus, the journey is incredible. John explains how all that works together:

> Dear friends, let us love one another, because love is from God, and everyone who loves has been born of God and knows God. The one who does not love does not know God, because God is love. God's love was revealed among us in this way: God sent His only Son into the world so that we might live through Him. Love consists in this: not that we loved God, but that He loved us and sent His Son to be the propitiation for our sins. Dear friends, if God loved us in this way, we also must love one another. No one has ever seen God. If we love one another, God remains in us and His love is perfected in us. This is how we know that we remain in Him and He in us: He has given to us from His Spirit. And we have seen and we testify that the Father has sent the Son as Savior of the world.
> —1 John 4:7–14

This overflowing love has three perspectives: *grace received, call obeyed,* and *neighbor served.* From God's perspective, His love is expressed in grace-filled initiative. The essence of love, John says, starts with the fact that God loved us and sent His Son to take on the punishment for our sins. His love leads you and me from sin and death to life.

From our perspective back to God, we love Him because He first loved us. How does God want us to love Him? With all that we have—with our heart, our soul, our mind, and all our strength (Mark 12:30). In simplest terms, this love overflowing from us back to God takes on the form of obedience to Him. "For this is what love for God is: to keep His commands" (1 John 5:3). God's overflowing love enables us to live out—to obey—a call He has for each of us, because we know that He will provide all that we need.

But there is a necessary third perspective of this overflowing love: from our perspective toward other people. Simply put, "If God loved us in this way, we also must love one another"

(1 John 4:11). What incredible freedom we have that comes with loving Him! We have the freedom to receive a depth of love that no one else can give us. This deep, unfathomable love frees us to love others in a manner that brings them joy. This love also frees us to love ourselves as we *are*—far from perfect.

Grace Received: Another Leper Discovers God's Grace

God's grace is revolutionary because of the many ways it touches our lives. It saves us (Ephesians 2:8). It forgives us (Isaiah 43:25). It sustains us (Philippians 2:13). It heals our broken hearts (Psalm 147:3). It liberates us from condemnation and legalism (Romans 8:1). It transforms us (Romans 12:2). It matures us (2 Peter 3:18). From beginning to end in our encounters with God in this life, we never stop experiencing His overflowing love in the form of grace. The Apostle Paul described it this way as he approached the latter years of his life and ministry: "But I count my life of no value to myself, so that I may finish my course and the ministry I received from the Lord Jesus, *to testify to the gospel of God's grace*" (Acts 20:24; emphasis mine).

God's grace often comes from unexpected sources.

I have seen those with leprosy firsthand, and this experience draws my attention to an Old Testament story of a man from a pagan nation who had a surprising encounter with God and His grace. In 2 Kings 5, Naaman experienced the same grace and overflowing love that my Thai friend did those many years ago. I see God's grace at work throughout this man's experience. Let me give you a bit of background. The Book of 1 Kings records the division of God's people and land into two kingdoms—Israel and Judah. Israel was the Northern Kingdom, made up of ten tribes. Judah and Benjamin became known as the Southern Kingdom. Sometimes during past political campaigns here in the United States, I have said, "I'm voting for the lesser of two evils." That didn't happen in Israel. First Kings tells of 8 kings in Israel and their reigns—*all* were evil! Read 2 Kings, and you will find 11 more administrations; *all* evil except one—Shallum—and he reigned only one month! In 2 Kings, we see the confrontation between Elisha and an army commander.

The first ten chapters of 2 Kings describe the Elisha's ministry, a diverse ministry as noted by the frequency and variety of the 17 miracles he performed. Midway through Elisha's ministry, Naaman's story appears.

> Naaman, commander of the army for the king of Aram, was a great man in his master's sight and highly regarded because through him, the LORD had given victory to Aram. The man was a brave warrior, but he had a skin disease. Aram had gone on raids and brought back from the land of Israel a young girl who served Naaman's wife. She said to her mistress, "If only my master would go to the prophet who is in Samaria, he would cure him of his skin disease." So Naaman went and told his master what the girl from the land of Israel had said. Therefore, the king of Aram said, "Go and I will send a letter with you to the king of Israel."
> —2 Kings 5:1–5

Like many notable people, Naaman had a lot going for him. He was in a position of great influence and authority as the commander of the army. He was highly regarded by the king of Aram. He had been an instrument of God's judgment against Israel's armies. And Naaman was a valiant soldier. But Naaman had a big problem—he had leprosy. And he was destined for a surprising encounter with the grace of God.

God's grace often comes from unexpected sources. Here the instrument of His grace was a servant girl—an Israelite who had been taken into slavery. Does it seem logical that she would be helping her captors? Logical? No. Gracious? Undoubtedly. Many of us have heard all our lives that grace is undeserved, unmerited favor. The slave girl's compassion is a demonstration of that. Under normal circumstances, this powerful, prestigious man of high position would hardly have looked to a slave girl as his source for help. But these weren't normal circumstances.

Naaman went to the king of Aram and told him of the prophet in Israel that could heal him. The king wrote a letter to the king of Israel asking for help. Naaman then set out for Israel with gold, silver, and fine clothes to pay for the cure. He was in for another surprise.

> He brought the letter to the king of Israel, and it read: "When this letter comes to you, note that I have sent you my servant Naaman for you to cure him of his skin disease." When the king of Israel read the letter, he tore his clothes and asked, "Am I God, killing and giving life that this man expects me to cure a man of his skin disease? Think it over and you will see that he is only picking a fight with me." When Elisha the man of God heard that the king of Israel tore his clothes, he sent a message to the king, "Why have you torn your clothes? Have him come to me, and he will know there is a prophet in Israel." So Naaman came with his horses and chariots and stood at the door of Elisha's house.
> —2 Kings 5:6–9

Have you experienced God's love and grace that seemed disguised at the time as something else? Problems? Impossible situations? Threats? People don't always understand God's grace. Joram, the wicked king of Israel, surely didn't. His reaction to Naaman and the Aramean king's letter make it clear that he misunderstood the intent. Joram tore his clothes in grief because he thought Aram was looking for an excuse to attack Israel. But this was all part of God's plan—even though he couldn't understand it. Enter God's instrument of grace—Elisha—who says to the king, "Send him to me!" Both the king of Israel and the champion of Aram would learn that impossible situations come loaded with potential for God's matchless grace.

Potential, because that grace must be accepted, and on God's terms. Naaman thought Elisha would be impressed by his visit. After all, he was a man of great power, position, and prestige. If Elisha were not impressed by Naaman, then surely he would be impressed by all the treasures Naaman brought with him—the gold, the silver, and the magnificent clothing. Naaman knew how things worked! He'd been around the block a few times. But he met his match with the servant of the Lord, and discovered that God will not be manipulated into doing what we want.

Then Elisha sent him a messenger, who said, "Go wash seven times in the Jordan and your flesh will be restored and you will be clean." But Naaman got angry and left, saying, "I was telling myself: He will surely come out, stand and call on the name of Yahweh his God, and will wave his hand over the spot and cure the skin disease. Aren't Abana and Pharpar, the rivers of Damascus, better than all the waters of Israel? Could I not wash in them and be clean?" So he turned and left in a rage. But his servants approached and said to him, "My father, if the prophet had told you to do some great thing, would you not have done it? How much more should you do it when he tells you, 'Wash and be clean'?" So Naaman went down and dipped himself in the Jordan seven times, according to the command of the man of God. Then his skin was restored and became like the skin of a small boy, and he was clean.

—2 Kings 5:13–14

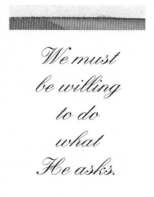

We must be willing to do what He asks.

Elisha did not even meet him at the door, but sent a messenger instead. Naaman flew into a rage. He was disappointed and angry that Elisha didn't do some grand external act. And on top of that, the prophet had told Naaman to wash in the dirty Jordan River. Come on! So he stomped away.

Yet again, it was a servant who saved the day. Naaman's servants reasoned with him: "If the prophet would have asked you to do something great, you would have done it. Why not give this a try?"

And after his anger subsided, Naaman headed off to the Jordan. We can't lose sight of what an act of humility this was for this rich, famous, powerful man who enjoyed his life of status to lower himself into the dirty water of the Jordan. But such an act of humility was necessary for his healing. It's still necessary.

As people of God, we need to remember that "God resists the proud, but gives grace to the humble" (James 4:6). Without God, all the gold and silver in the world cannot help us, whatever our pedigree, calling, status, or natural abilities. We must be willing to do what He asks—even when it doesn't make sense to us.

Call Obeyed

Author Os Guinness writes in his book *The Call,* "Calling is the truth that God calls us to himself so decisively that everything we are, everything we do, and everything we have is...lived out as a response to his summons and service." The prophet Jeremiah experienced such a calling that the Lord said came before his birth:

> The word of the LORD came to me:
> I chose you before I formed you in the womb;
> I set you apart before you were born.
> I appointed you a prophet to the nations.
> —Jeremiah 1:4–5

> Jeremiah would later testify of God's love that calls us to Himself:
> I have loved you with an everlasting love; therefore,
> I have continued to extend faithful love to you.
> —Jeremiah 31:3

Everything I see and do as a Christian is filtered by my experience of growing up on the missions field in Thailand. I watched my mother and father be instruments of God's grace to the people they loved so dearly. But as I mentioned earlier, what kept them going was an unmistakable sense of God's calling on their lives as medical missionaries. But even as a little girl, I was certain that God's grace and love had called me too. Over the years, His call has taken on different forms. Sometimes it was loud and clear, and my life changed direction accordingly. At other times the voice of the Lord has been quiet and still. In my heart and mind I have found myself asking, "Was that You, Lord?"

"Asking me to do *what*?"

"Are you *sure*?"

"Who, *me,* Lord?"

Do you wonder if you have ever heard His call? We who have received Christ as our Savior have. Some callings are shared by all believers, although these callings may have different expressions.

For example, all of us are called to be missionaries in some way. For me, that started alongside my parents. Each day, they instilled in me the urgency of needing to bring light to dark places to those who have never even heard Jesus's name in their own language. And God has sent other models who have encouraged me and many others. Some of us may never be called to live overseas, but we are called to missionary action in our realms of influence.

We each have a circle of influence.

We each have a circle of influence— people who look to us for reasons, direction, and decision making. God is calling all of us to be people of influence for *Him*. He is calling us to walk worthy of our calling (Ephesians 4:1). To walk as Jesus walked, live as He lived. To live God's call means to walk in His way, to be a difference maker. He has called all of us to understand and to embrace the call, and then to walk worthy as we live the call He has placed on our lives.

Our greatest example of a person of influence, of course, is Jesus. Think with me for a moment about the relationship between Jesus, the disciples, and the women who followed Him (Luke 8:1–3). What kind of influence did Jesus have on their lives during the three short years they were together? What kind of impact on the world did He have through the Twelve, along with the women whom He influenced? Jesus taught them Scripture, how to pray, and how to minister. And in one of the last experiences Jesus had with His disciples, He tried one last time to influence how they would live their lives. By washing the disciples' feet (John 13:1–15), He demonstrated that an influential person serves. Those examples of influence which Jesus modeled speak to the callings of every believer.

At other times, however, God's call is unique to us. He calls us to form new realms of influence intentionally, and to express His love in ways completely unique to us. For example, God called me to be a nurse. And for this missionary kid in Thailand, this meant returning to the United States to go to nursing school. Although it was the country of my birth, the United States had become a strange place where I knew virtually no one.

I arrived for college at Baylor University. My grandparents dropped me at the door to my room. There I sat on a twin bed in a very bare room and cried. I knew no one. I had only my clothes brought from Thailand. Everything I owned was in a suitcase. I watched other students carrying all the comforts they needed to make a dorm room a home, including matching bedspreads. I was overwhelmed with loneliness. I knew no one there and only knew my grandparents and a few relatives in the United States. I was so homesick that, as I sat on my bed, I desperately wanted to go home to Thailand. I prayed and prayed. I knew God had called me to be there and I was to obey Him. But the loneliness was almost more than I could bear. I always knew I needed the Lord, but on this day that took on a profound new meaning. He was all I had, and I realized *He was all that I needed.* His overwhelming, overflowing love covered me in waves of love and assurance.

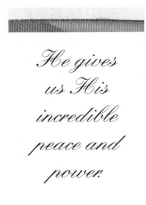

He gives us His incredible peace and power.

Near the end of the day, I was still in that bare, empty room, when the Lord sent me a special gift. Unknown to me, my best friend *in fifth grade* had requested me as a roommate. We had met when my family was home on furlough (now stateside assignment). My childhood friend knew I would be coming back to the States and she picked me! Her mother came in, hauling everything needed for our room—for both of us. God showed me *His* love through a measure of grace in my life when I was so lonely through a roommate and her mom including me in the plans for the room, providing me things for the room, and sticking to me like a sister. His love and provision for me as I followed His call amazed me. I knew His love was enough to overcome all the obstacles that I would face.

But the Lord extended His grace one step further, beyond my roommate and her mother. A local woman, "Aunt Ann," took me under her wing. She and her husband were former missionaries to Nigeria. He was a physician and had retired to Waco, where he had a practice. Aunt Ann found out I was coming and knew how hard it was for MKs to adjust to a different culture. Part of their "love overflowing" ministry was to help me, as well as other returning MKs, slowly reimmerse ourselves into American culture. They took me shopping, helped me open a bank account, taught me to drive, and stood in for my parents on parents weekend at Baylor.

The point to all this is that while your call from God is unique in some ways, it is never alone or in isolation. Jeremiah protested when the Lord called him to be a prophet. "Oh no, Lord God! Look, I don't know how to speak since I am only a youth" (Jeremiah 1:6).

The Lord's reply speaks to our callings as well:

Do not say: I am only a youth,
for you will go to everyone I send you to
and speak whatever I tell you.
Do not be afraid of anyone,
for *I will be with you to deliver you.*
This is the Lord's declaration.
—Jeremiah 1:7–8 (emphasis mine)

Jeremiah was very young. I was in a strange country where I knew no one and had nothing beyond what was in a suitcase. What makes *you* feel isolated, intimidated, or alone? Remember, following God's call means following *God*! It's personal. And you are never alone. The best He has to offer is ours for the taking—if we only would! He gives us His incredible presence and power as His call draws us to His design. Will you be a person of influence? Are you listening to His call for you? Don't let your fear or your pain keep you from the joy of following His call.

Neighbor Served

The third dimension of God's overflowing love is neighbor to neighbor. While we express love to God through worship and obedience, we communicate love for others by meeting needs. In speaking of the Greatest Commandment to love God with all our hearts, Jesus hastened to add, "The second is like it: you shall love your neighbor as yourself" (Matthew 22:39). One of the greatest ways to express God's love and respond to His call is to embrace the needs of the people right in front of you. As a wife, mother, and now grandmother, I have an opportunity daily to display to people closest to me that God loves them. As a leader in my church, I have had the opportunity to touch children's and teenagers' lives and show them that their lives and destinies matter to God and to the world. As the president of a missions organization, I have the opportunity to help believers be relevant and radically involved in the mission of God. At any given time, my "neighbor" may be my daughter, grandson, a teenager at my church, or an international missionary. While the opportunities appear in different forms, the call to love others with Christ's love is very consistent.

In describing why he was so motivated to share the gospel with unbelievers, Paul said simply, "Christ's love compels us" (2 Corinthians 5:14). Bill Hyde understood what that meant.

A church planter in the southern Philippines, Bill started hundreds of churches, traveling to some of the remotest areas of Mindanao. He was a servant leader. Filipinos would often ask Bill why he stayed in the Philippines, where it was so hot and so hard to live. Bill would always give the same answer: "Because I love Filipinos."

Five years before Bill was due to retire, he went to the Davao City airport to pick up a missionary couple coming back from Manila. While waiting outside, a bomb hidden in a backpack a few feet away from Bill exploded. He was killed almost instantly. Because of his size, his body blocked the blast from hitting Filipinos who were standing around him. In essence, he died so that many others could live. Thousands of Filipinos came for his memorial service. At the bomb site where Bill died, someone placed a wreath with this inscription: "In honor of Bill Hyde who along with other Americans think Filipinos are worth dying for." Bill loved his neighbors, even in death.

Another young missionary couple, in their early 30s and parents of two small boys, was called to the Middle East. The entire family fell in love with the country God had called them to. At the end of their first term, the husband had a cough that wouldn't go away. He had been to the doctor, who suspected that he was simply reacting to the dust and fatigue. Once they arrived stateside for furlough (now stateside assignment), however, the cough was still there. He went to the doctor, expecting to find out he had allergies or something simple. Instead, he discovered he had lung cancer in both lungs. His wife was expecting their third child, and the prognosis suggested he would not live to see that baby born. He didn't want to spend his final days in North America, but with the people to whom he had been called. His mission board could not allow him to return permanently, but he was allowed to return for some months. Every day he went out on the streets and talked to Arab after Arab about the true God and Christ. Then they learned that he had returned in spite of his cancer. This touched the Arab people, and many came to know Christ. When he returned to the United States to await his impending death, God was gracious and allowed him to live long enough to see his third child born. Even in the face of a shortened life, he was faithful to love the people God had called him to—his beloved Arab people and his family.

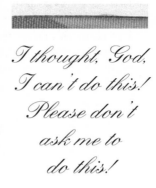

I thought, God, I can't do this! Please don't ask me to do this!

Most of us will not be required to love to the extent that it costs our physical lives. But we will have to love enough to be willing to give up our own desires, time, preferences, schedules, and much more. But that is a small price because we are loved by someone who thought we were worth dying for—Jesus Christ.

This came home to me in a particularly poignant way in my responsibilities as an intensive care nurse. I heard God's call loud and clear as He called me to work with the leprosy of our day. I will never forget the first time I cared for a patient with AIDS. I thought, *God, I can't do this! I have a family—small children who need me. Please don't ask me to do this!* (I knew in my head, of course, that I couldn't get AIDS from just being in the room.) I stood outside the door to the room of my first AIDS patient for what seemed like an eternity, just praying: "Lord, what do I do?" Then I remembered what Jesus did, and what my father did. They willingly, lovingly, touched the lepers of their day. I could do no less.

I inhaled deeply and opened the door—to see the smiling face of a two-year-old. A little boy who didn't ask for this—who didn't know he was an outcast with a dreaded disease. From then on, I never looked back.

The love God gives is the overflowing kind. The more you and I are willing to receive from Him, offer back to Him, and to share with others, the more greatly we can be a conduit of that love that changed the world forever. In the next chapter, I want to introduce you to someone who seemed to know instinctively how to express her love to Jesus, regardless of the setting.

For Reflection and Discussion

1. Like the paraffin bath, children often make adult tools objects of adventure. What kinds of adventures did you have when you were a child?

2. Read Ephesians 2:8–9. How would you define grace? Why would someone who had received God's grace be more inclined to love others?

3. Read Ephesians 4:1. There Paul speaks of a "calling" on every believer. What does calling mean to you? How does God's call make you just like every other believer, and how does it make you unique?

4. It may well be that our most desperately needed answers arrive in surprising packages, such as happened to Naaman. Who might *you* be overlooking? Who may God want to use to bless you?

5. Read 2 Corinthians 5:14. Have you ever felt "compelled" by God's love to serve or express love for someone else? Give an example.

6. Tell your own story of "grace received, call obeyed, or neighbor served." How has God's love touched your life with His grace and/or overflowed to someone else?

Chapter 2

The Love Before All Else

I'm not Supergirl.

Krystal Harris isn't either, but she describes what many of us feel. Her hit song from the 2001 movie *The Princess Diaries* describes what many of us feel: "I'm supergirl," she said, "and I'm here to save the world." But a haunting question lingers: "Who's gonna save me?"

Sometimes we Christians make the mistake of assuming that the purpose of books and studies such as this one is to turn us into Supergirl or her male counterpart. Instead of a magic piano, we may look to our magic gift of speech. Our magic home or family. Our magic talent or hard work. *Called to love?* No problem. I'll simply learn a new technique, work harder, or squeeze another half hour into my already hopelessly busy day.

Jesus offers us a better, more eternally significant way. He asks us to *love Him first*. When asked by a Bible expert (something of a Superman of his day) what the greatest commandment in the Law was, Jesus replied without hesitation, *"Love the Lord your God* with all your heart, with all your soul, and with all your mind" (Matthew 22:37; emphasis mine). You and I can't possibly love our neighbors as ourselves until we establish and protect our first love for the Lord.

The same principle applies to groups or congregations. The New Testament church at Ephesus was something of a "superchurch." Paul had spent a significant amount of time there (1 Corinthians 16:8–9). When he wrote to the Ephesians, he said things to them he didn't say to any other church.

> This is why, since I heard about your faith in the Lord Jesus and your love for all the saints, I never stop giving thanks for you as I remember you in my prayers. I pray that the God of our Lord Jesus Christ, the glorious Father, would give you a spirit of wisdom and revelation in the knowledge of Him. I pray that the eyes of your heart may be enlightened so you may know what is the hope of His calling, what are the glorious riches of His inheritance among the saints, and what is the immeasurable greatness of His power to us who believe, according to the working of His vast strength.
> —Ephesians 1:15–19

These people were special. Their faith in Christ and their love for other believers throughout the world gave them a reputation. This prompted Paul to pray a rich prayer for them—a prayer for revelation, wisdom, and deeper understanding of the incredibly glorious wealth they shared in Christ.

This superchurch appears again some 35 years after Paul wrote the words above. This time, the Lord Jesus Himself is sending the message. At first it appears similar. The church at Ephesus was still a vibrant hub of activity and work. What pastor or church leader wouldn't want to hear these words:

> I know your works, your labor, and your endurance, and that you cannot tolerate evil. You have tested those who call themselves apostles and are not, and you have found them to be liars. You also possess endurance and have tolerated many things because of My name, and have not grown weary.
> —Revelation 2:2–3

Called to Love

Unfortunately, however, Jesus didn't stop there. Somehow in their efforts to do all and to be all, these believers had forgotten—abandoned—their first love.

> But I have this against you: you have abandoned the love you had at first. Remember then how far you have fallen; repent, and do the works you did at first. Otherwise, I will come to you and remove your lampstand from its place—unless you repent.
> —Revelation 2:4–5

In this chapter, we will look at someone who understood first love. In fact, she may have been the only person during the ministry of Jesus who actually *did* understand it—disciples included. Unlike her quiet brother and Supergirl sister, Mary of Bethany possessed a love for Jesus that transcended activity, doctrine, and charity. She understood Him and His mission as no one else did. She expressed love and trust toward Him more powerfully and consistently

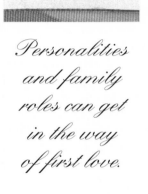

Personalities and family roles can get in the way of first love.

than anyone else. And in so doing, she modeled for generations to come the love before all other loves. The three scenes in which she appears in the Gospels reveal three expressions of first love: focused attention, extravagant worship, and total trust.

Focused Attention

Mary never appears in the Gospels without her sister Martha close by. They always approached situations differently because they obviously had different personalities and family roles. But sometimes, as in our first introduction to these sisters, personalities and family roles can get in the way of first love.

> While they were traveling, He entered a village, and a woman named Martha welcomed Him into her home. She had a sister named Mary, who also sat at the Lord's feet and was listening to what He said. But Martha was

distracted by her many tasks, and she came up and asked, "Lord, don't You care that my sister has left me to serve alone? So tell her to give me a hand."

The Lord answered her, "Martha, Martha, you are worried and upset about many things, but one thing is necessary. Mary has made the right choice, and it will not be taken away from her."
—Luke 10:38–42

Jesus was coming to their house, and Martha wanted everything to be just right. She was a perfectionist. Everyone who knew her knew that she was disciplined, strong-willed, energetic, and practical. She knew who she was and where she was going. She was a leader in her day and people listened to her! Probably Martha was single, financially secure, and owned her own home, which she shared with Mary and their brother, Lazarus. Some think that "Simon the [ex-] leper" may have been the father of the three (Matthew 26:6). Evidently Martha had the gift of hospitality and entertained often, freely welcoming friends as well as strangers to their home. Everyone knew they had an open invitation to stay there. Yet in her busyness and desire to make it all right, she forgot her most important goal, and her most significant Guest. Like the Ephesians, she was enduring and serving, but had forgotten why.

In her distraction and frustration, Supergirl burst into the room. "Lord, don't You care that my sister has left me to serve alone? So tell her to give me a hand" (Luke 10:40). Jack Deere comments in *Surprised by the Voice of God*:

> Martha wasn't really asking the Lord a question. She was using a question to express her anger with the Lord. Like the time your little brother asked you, "Why are you so stupid?" He wasn't waiting for an explanation of genetics in heredity. He was expressing his anger toward you. Distraction makes us oblivious to the presence of the Lord. And when we try to serve God without his presence we become angry and bitter with him and his servants. We also try to use the Lord to control others—"Tell her to help me." Distraction can even lead to the arrogance of commanding God.

At any given time, we can make the same mistake Martha made. It's not about personalities or life circumstances. It's about forgetting what (and who) is most important. Martha's action became distraction. In her attempt to satisfy her own expectations of what a good hostess should be, she neglected the best—that the Son of God was seated in her home, making Himself available to her. Her busyness and fatigue led her to question Jesus's heart.

Martha was frustrated when Jesus didn't see what she saw—when He didn't get frustrated by what frustrated her. "Don't you care?" she asked. We sometimes have the same frustrations. "Lord, don't You care that I'm trying to save money and my spouse is trying to spend it? Tell him or her to stop." "Lord, don't You care that I'm trying to have a clean home and my kids are slobs? Tell them to straighten up." "Lord, don't You care that I'm trying to do this (whatever 'this' is) right, and I'm the only one? Tell the rest of the world to get their act together."

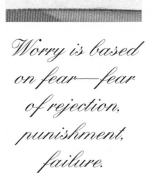

Worry is based on fear—fear of rejection, punishment, failure.

Martha was frustrated with Mary because Mary was making her look bad. Jesus also used the word *bothered* to describe her. She was so uptight, she became resentful, both toward Mary and toward Jesus. Her attention to the "many things" (Luke 10:41) led her to neglect the "one thing." Jesus's kind rebuke to Martha had a chilling undertone: *"Martha, this isn't about you.* It isn't about what kind of hostess you are, about what kind of house you live in, or about what kind of home you run. Today it's about Me, and Mary gets it."

Jesus referred to Martha as "worried." Worry is based on fear—fear of rejection, fear of failure, fear of punishment. She was trying to do everything possible to please others. She was trying to please the Lord Jesus and the disciples and probably those who followed Jesus around. She couldn't even stop to think about what was happening around her because she was so busy doing it all. It wasn't her *service* Jesus rebuked, but her fearful attitude. Later (John 12:2) you can find her serving with the right perspective, and it made all the difference of the world! Jesus wants us to use our gifts and talents, but only as expression of love for Him first.

So where was Mary? She was where Jesus was. She wanted to hear every word He said. She didn't want to miss a thing He had to say. Was she lazy? I don't think so. She just wanted to sit by Jesus and, offering Him her undivided attention, soak it all up. Mary was completely different from her sister. She lived for those higher moments in life. She exhibited a free spirit and strong individualism. Mary probably saw little value in material wealth, a clean house, and cooked meals. I think she was an avid learner who thrived on anything that compelled her to think and reflect.

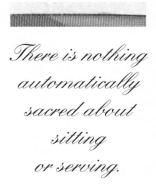

There is nothing automatically sacred about sitting or serving.

Mary was almost childlike in her hunger for truth—especially spiritual truth—and like her sister, she felt things deeply. She did several things that were not the norm. She sat with the men who sat with Jesus—a violation of custom in those days. She was lost in the presence of Jesus, and didn't mind that the men were talking about her. She wanted to know Jesus. Mary was brave. To be so boldly unconventional was daring. But she didn't care what others thought about her. Mary was just as human and imperfect as Martha, but while Martha was busy *serving* Jesus, Mary was in the living room, *enjoying* Him.

Every relationship, including your relationship with Christ, involves a tension between talking and doing on one end, and resting and listening on the other. There is nothing automatically sacred about sitting *or* serving. What makes either of those activities special is the degree to which Jesus has your attention in the midst of it. At any given time, either Mary or Martha could have chosen either; in fact, Jesus makes a point that the difference between them was that Mary *chose* the better part (Luke 10:42). Mary chose to listen first. That's how first love responds. Leanne Payne comments in *Listening Prayer*:

> Sometimes when we most need to hear God speak the word comes when we are least inclined to listen. This listening, though it saves lives in every sense of the word,

is most needed to remove hazards from the crucial work of the kingdom. This listening helps us do the will of God. When Jesus visited the home of Martha and Mary, this is what Mary did. She silenced her soul and sat in obedience at Jesus' feet to hear his every word.

Even in an intensely busy situation, Mary chose the best. She offered her devotion and friendship to Jesus as a matter of choice and focus. She kept her attention on Him even when life around her was incredibly distracting. She loved Him, even in an environment of anger and resentment. She gave herself permission to do everything else imperfectly, so long as she loved Him completely. And she came to Him boldly, without fear of rejection or the disapproval of others. Jack Deere says in *Surprised by the Voice of God*:

> Mary is the kind of friend Jesus is seeking. She would rather sit at his feet and listen to him than anything else in the world. She doesn't want anything from him other than his presence. Mary wanted to hear the voice of Jesus because to her it was the sweetest voice in all the world. She wanted to see his face because it was, to her, the most lovely of all faces. She simply wanted Jesus, and Jesus was enough for her. Being with him satisfied every need and every desire she had ever experienced. She was his friend. He was her friend. And Jesus shares his secrets with his friends.

In any given situation, busy or passive, you, like the Bethany sisters, have the opportunity to choose the best. It comes back to the choice to give and receive love. Does Jesus have *your* attention right now? Have you learned to still yourself, to listen to His words, to enjoy His company with no agenda? That's first love.

Extravagant Worship

No one would ever have accused Charles Wesley of being casual in His relationship to the Lord Jesus. Over a 50-year span, he wrote approximately 6,500 songs of praise to God. This "undignified lover of God," as he is called by Matt Redman in his book *The Unquenchable Worshipper*, used a foolish picture to express his great gratitude for the gift of salvation. On the first anniversary of becoming a Christian, Wesley wrote, "O for a thousand tongues to sing my great Redeemer's praise." He was lavish in his exuberance of worship, and looked for extraordinary ways to express it.

Growing up on the missions field has given me a different

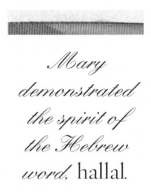

Mary demonstrated the spirit of the Hebrew word, hallal.

perspective on worship. When I returned to the States, it seemed that so much of "worship" was wrapped up in what type of church building, what style of music, or how long the sermon lasted, instead of time with the Lord. Worship is not a thing or an event. It should be a constant state that we are in—praising God, praying, and listening to His Word. God desires for us to be one with Him; worship is the way we express to Him that we love Him with all that we have and are. That requires integrated lives, and that's not easy. It's hard to integrate all the parts of your life into one focused life that loves the Lord. We tend to separate and compartmentalize our work, personal, social, and church lives. But if we love the Lord, we will love Him at work, at play, and at home. We'll even love Him when we're out to dinner.

Six days before the Passover, Jesus came to Bethany where Lazarus was, whom Jesus had raised from the dead. So they gave a dinner for Him there; Martha was serving them, and Lazarus was one of those reclining at the table with Him. Then Mary took a pound of fragrant oil—pure and expensive nard—anointed Jesus' feet, and wiped His feet with her hair. So the house was filled with the fragrance of the oil.

Then one of His disciples, Judas Iscariot (who was about to betray Him), said, "Why wasn't this fragrant oil sold for 300 denarii and given to the poor?" He didn't say this because he cared about the poor but because he was a thief. He was in charge of the money-bag and would steal part of what was put in it.

Called to Love

Jesus answered, "Leave her alone; she has kept it for the day of My burial. For you always have the poor with you, but you do not always have Me."
—John 12:1–8

From scene to scene, Mary has gone from a woman who listens quietly to one who worships lavishly. The nard that John referred to was made from dried leaves of a rare Himalayan plant. It was rare and expensive enough that it could have fed an entire meal to hundreds of families. How much do *you* earn in a year? This perfume was worth nearly that much. And the alabaster jar (Mark 14:3) was in itself an expensive thing of beauty.

First love prompted Mary to give generously and sacrificially in her worship. Giving has been a component of worship ever since it was first instituted. The Lord instructed Moses in Exodus 34:20: "No one is to appear before Me empty-handed." But there are those unique times when, in love and devotion, He is pleased for us to "break our alabaster jars" and offer our finest to Him. Charles Swindoll writes in *Living Above the Level of Mediocrity*:

> There are certain times when extravagance is appropriate. In our day of emphasis on high-tech calculations and finely tuned budgets with persistent reminders of cost, restraint, and propriety, ... anything beyond the basics can be misconstrued as excessive. If you buy into that ever-present Spartan philosophy, then everything you build will be functional, ordinary, and basic. Everything you purchase will be at the lowest cost. Everything you do will be average.

Mary also demonstrates a remarkable lack of self-awareness. She again ignores the propriety of her culture that forbade women from approaching men reclining at a table. Then, with the stunning fragrance of the perfume permeating the air, she further surprised them all by letting down her hair and using it to wipe perfume on Jesus's feet. Author Hal Lindsey, in *Combat Faith*, refers to this as the "gaiety of abandoned praise. With glorious imprudence she broke the container and with loving care used the whole contents. She was liberated out of herself in a dramatic devotion." Mary demonstrated the spirit of the Hebrew word, *hallal*, from which we get the word *hallelujah*. One might suggest that it "means to be clamorishly foolish or mad before the Lord," according to Matt Redman in *The Unquenchable Worshipper*. As we are more object centered in our love for Jesus, like Mary, we will be less aware of ourselves and others' opinions about us.

This event took place shortly before Jesus's crucifixion, and He made it clear that Mary understood something no one else did. Time after time, Jesus had warned His disciples that He was destined for a cross and death. Yet they never seemed to grasp His meaning. At least to Judas, and perhaps to others (Mark 14:4), His ministry had become a business and a social project. But to Mary, Jesus was even then her *Savior*. She understood that everything— even her love for Him as He reclined at a dinner table—pointed to the reason He came in the first place.

Total Trust

One morning Monica got up and found that it was hard to reach up into a cabinet. She had not been feeling well that week, and it was getting worse. By nightfall she was a quadriplegic and not expected to live. Monica, a vibrant woman, loved the Lord and lived each day serving Him in her native state of Arkansas. She remained unconscious on life support for weeks. Slowly she became somewhat stable, although she remained on life support. On the outside of her door in the intensive care unit, she had a sign placed that said, *"I serve a Risen Lord; inquire within for details."*

What an impossible situation. Monica was unable to move anything but her head. Nevertheless, day after day she continued to minister and be a witness to the staff and to those families around her who were hurting. Once visitors were in the door, she would use a word board and mouth pen to tell them about Jesus. It would have been easy for her to be angry and bitter at God and want to die. But she used this as an opportunity to show others His love for her and for them. This was an impossible situation, but yet she completely trusted God for everything. Because she had no control over anything from the neck down, she had to give Him all the control for things that we normally take for granted.

Missionaries also understand the concept of trusting God in difficult situations. They are great examples of loving the Lord and obeying Him when it is difficult. They leave all that they have and go to another place to love the people in that culture. They often leave aging parents behind; often they will not see them again or be able to help as they age. Missionaries leave grandchildren behind instead of being involved in their lives—they see them every few years. They love the Lord so much, they are willing to take their children into dangerous places in order to share the love of Jesus with those that don't know Him.

Now, four days after his death, Jesus had arrived.

You can see that same type of faith in Mary. Unlike previous examples, Mary didn't always understand—but she always seemed to trust Jesus completely. John 11 records the experience of the sickness and death of her brother, Lazarus. Martha had sent for Jesus, but Lazarus had died in the meantime. Now, four days after his death, Jesus had arrived.

> Having said this, she went back and called her sister Mary, saying in private, "The Teacher is here and is calling for you."
>
> As soon as she heard this, she got up quickly and went to Him. Jesus had not yet come into the village but was still in the place where Martha had met Him. The Jews who were with her in the house consoling her saw that Mary got up quickly and went out. So they followed her, supposing that she was going to the tomb to cry there.
>
> When Mary came to where Jesus was and saw Him, she fell at His feet and told Him, "Lord, if You had been here, my brother would not have died!"
>
> When Jesus saw her crying, and the Jews who had come with her crying, He was angry in His spirit and deeply moved. "Where have you put him?" He asked.
>
> "Lord," they told Him, "come and see."
>
> Jesus wept.

—John 11:28–35

Again, this story contrasts Mary and her sister Martha. This time, however, it is in a time of grief. Martha had immediately run toward Jesus when she heard He was approaching town, while Mary waited to be called (John 11:20). Martha's exclamation, "Lord, if you had been here, my brother wouldn't have died" (John 11:21), led to a discussion about death, the Resurrection, and who Jesus was. At worst, it was an argument. At best, Martha was growing in her faith and trying to understand.

Mary was hurting too. But even in her grief, her love for Jesus shone through. All she had to hear was that Jesus had approached the village and wanted to see her, and Mary ran to meet Him. Even though her heart was broken, she displayed a first-love attitude that said, "Lord, You're here now, and that's all that matters!"

What Jesus wanted to demonstrate to both sisters was that all they hoped for was found in Him—even if it appeared He hadn't come through as they had wanted. In her grief, Martha had expressed disappointment that Jesus didn't get there on time. Can you relate?

"Your brother will rise again," Jesus told her (John 11:23).

Martha believed that, as a point of doctrine. "I know that he will rise again in the resurrection at the last day," she said (John 11:24).

But Jesus pressed in. He wanted Martha to see and experience something so personally profound, it would change forever how she viewed life and death, love and loss. "I am the resurrection and the life. The one who believes in Me, even if he dies, will live. Everyone who lives and believes in Me will never die—ever. Do you believe this?" (John 11:25–26).

Martha had her theology straight. She knew that *someday* there would be a resurrection. What she didn't understand was that she was talking to Him! "Yes, Lord," she told Him, "I believe You are the Messiah, the Son of God, who was to come into the world" (John 11:27).

Into the world! That's correct, Martha. But Jesus wanted her (and us) to see Him on a much more personal level than this. Martha had a saving faith in Jesus, that He was the Son of God, sent to the world. What she needed was a faith that Jesus was at that minute sent to *her*! To *her* pain. To *her* unanswered questions. To *her* impossible situation. To give *her* victory over defeat and despair. She understood to a point. Jesus wanted her to experience something much greater. His reply?

"Go get Mary" (John 11:28).

"Lord, if you had been here, my brother would not have died" (John 11:32). Mary used the exact same language. But His response was totally different. Maybe it was in the tone in her voice or her body language. Maybe it was more in contrast with the herd of mourners (and Jesus critics) who followed her, thinking she was going to the tomb. But even in her sorrow, Mary had a faith that assumed a familiar position. She fell at His feet. There, she completely submitted herself in faith to Jesus, whether the circumstances made sense to her or not. Mary got it.

It's one thing to be at Jesus's feet when He is teaching. It's another thing to be at His feet when your heart is broken.

Focused attention, extravagant love, and total trust. That is what *first love* looks like. We never hear from Mary again. True to her quiet nature, we are left to assume she lived out her days in love with a then risen Christ. But even for Mary there were no guarantees. First love requires renewal, attentiveness, and diligence.

Only when we love Jesus with *all* of our heart, soul, mind, and strength can we offer that same kind of love to others. But when we do offer Him our passion, our being, and our strength—not with just part of it but with all of it—He gives us the amazing capacity to see through His eyes, to hear with His ears, to touch with His hands, to think with His mind, and to feel with His heart.

In other words, He frees us to love as He does. In the next part, we'll explore that more deeply.

For Reflection and Discussion

1. What are some "supergirl" images you have seen that put pressure on women (or men) to do everything perfectly?

2. Read Matthew 26:36–46. Like Martha, the disciples were distracted from focused attention on Christ. What are some things that can distract you?

3. Read Psalm 150. Have you ever seen someone worship God so lavishly or extravagantly that someone else questioned it as ridiculous? If yes, what did that person do? If no, what are some ways that *could* happen?

4. Read 2 Corinthians 12:7–10. Like Mary, Paul sometimes faced painful circumstances that required him to trust God's heart, even when he didn't understand at first. How has God challenged you in the past with the need to trust Him, even when it hurts?

5. Have you ever wished Jesus would "hurry up and get there," and been disappointed when He didn't respond like you wanted Him to?

6. How would you describe the state of your "first love" toward Jesus? Is it needing reviving, like Lazarus and the Ephesian church? Is it distracted, like Martha? Or is it focused and alive, like Mary?

Part 2

Take It In

"When He saw the crowds,
He felt compassion for them"
(Matthew 9:36).

When we look at things through love eyes, we're trying to
look and see as Jesus would see—beyond the immediate
physical or situational reality.

Chapter 3

Seeing with His Eyes

L ove eyes, please."
That has become something of a code in the Miller household.

Rachael, our daughter, had gone to the local fast-food drive-in. While she was there, she hit the ordering board and knocked the exterior mirror off the car. She cried all the way home, thinking Mark was going to be upset—even though she thinks she is the favorite child (they all do!). When she walked into the house, she cried and said she'd had a minor wreck. She asked her dad after he'd surveyed the damage to please to look at it—and her—through love eyes. "After all," she said plaintively, "I am the favorite."

Love eyes aren't limited to wrecks, blown curfews, bad grades, or parent-teacher conferences. On some days, after a long day of working in the yard and then doing some housecleaning (and looking like it), I'll be cooking dinner when Mark comes home from working all day. He'll walk over to me, give me a hug, and tell me how beautiful I look. Now I could slug him, but instead

I tell him that after 30 years of marriage, he has to be seeing me through love eyes. Or else he's blind! The truth is, those words mean more to me than anything he could say when I am all fixed up. I guess to my family, love eyes means looking at not what has happened or what someone looks like on the outside, but looking on the inside and seeing what *should* be seen. In short, it means giving grace because we love them.

You Are What You See

You and I live with complete consistency with the way we see ourselves, other people, our circumstances, and the Lord. In his book *The Ragamuffin Gospel*, Brennan Manning says:

> A person, in a real sense, is what he or she sees. And seeing depends on our eyes. Jesus uses the metaphor of eyes more often than that of minds or wills. The old proverb, "The eyes are the windows of the soul," contains a profound truth. Our eyes reveal whether our souls are spacious or cramped, hospitable or critical, compassionate or judgmental. The way we see other people is usually the way we see ourselves. If we have made peace with our flawed humanity and embraced our ragamuffin identity, we are able to tolerate in others what was previously unacceptable in ourselves.

Those eye metaphors Jesus used can be found throughout the Gospels. He called the eye the "lamp of the body." "If your eye is generous, your whole body will be full of light. But if your eye is stingy, your whole body will be full of darkness. So if the light within you is darkness—how deep is that darkness!" (Matthew 6:22–23).

In warning us against a spirit of criticism, Jesus cautioned against looking at the speck (fault) in your brother's eye, while remaining blind to the log in your own eye. "Hypocrite! First take the log out of your eye, and then you will see clearly to take the speck out of your brother's eye" (Matthew 7:5).

He explained to the disciples that He spoke in parables "because looking they do not see, and hearing they do not listen or understand" (Matthew 13:13). And in one of the most intriguing of

His miracles, Jesus took a blind man by the hand and brought him outside the village of Bethsaida. Spitting on his eyes and laying His hands on him, He asked the man, "Do you see anything?" The man looked up and replied, "I see people—they look to me like trees walking." Jesus responded by placing His hands on the man's eyes, and he saw clearly (Mark 8:22–26).

Many of us are at least figuratively like that partially healed blind man. We see people as if they may as well be trees. We see them in terms of their labels rather than in terms of God's love. Seeing through love eyes means looking beyond all the "stuff" on the outside—and seeing others for who they are. The kids often say that I'm looking at them through love eyes when I can express love to them when they have no makeup on, when they're grubby, when they are hurting, or most often, when they do something that doesn't please us. They would often say that I would look at other kids on missions trips with love eyes too. Everybody needs someone who can look past all the mess they're in or doing and see them for what they can be. That's what I mean by *love eyes*.

Everybody needs someone who can look past all the mess.

When we look at things through love eyes, we're trying to look and see as Jesus would see—beyond the immediate physical or situational reality. He saw beyond the multitudes of people to see real people with real needs. He looked beyond the peripheral things and saw their hurts and hearts. Matthew describes one such scene:

> Then Jesus went to all the towns and villages, teaching in their synagogues, preaching the good news of the kingdom, and healing every disease and every sickness. When He saw the crowds, He felt compassion for them, because they were weary and worn out, like sheep without a shepherd. Then He said to His disciples, "The harvest is abundant, but the workers are few. Therefore, pray to the Lord of the harvest to send out workers into His harvest."

Summoning His 12 disciples, He gave them authority over unclean spirits, to drive them out, and to heal every disease and every sickness.
—Matthew 9:35 to 10:1

Why did Jesus say the workers in the harvest were so few? Because they didn't see what Jesus saw. Visionless people see problems; Jesus, on the other hand, sees people and their needs. It's easy to get lost in labels, programs, buildings, or money and forget that all of those things represent people that Jesus loves. Those people are all unique, all needy in some way, and all part of God's redemptive plan.

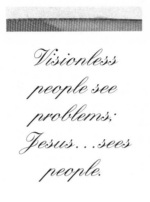

Visionless people see problems; Jesus...sees people.

The disciples, when they saw all those people, likely saw nothing more than confusion. In fact, they hardly ever handled large crowds well. Jesus, on the other hand, simply saw them as sheep that needed direction from a shepherd. That's how love eyes perceive ministry to people. These aren't circus lions that need a trainer. They aren't monkeys who need a cage and a little food once in a while. They are sheep, who need a fully engaged shepherd to guide and care for them.

While human nature tends to see the size of the job, Jesus saw the greatness of the potential when He looked at people. It's easy to see how big the harvest is, how far we have to go, and how much there is left undone. Through love eyes, Jesus saw how ripe the harvest was (and still is), and how much we can accomplish if we're faithful to the job. In spite of our complaints that something is wrong with the harvest, Jesus said that the reason we don't reap more of a harvest than we do is that there is no one to go get it.

Regardless of the condition of your vision, you can learn to see with the same kind of vision and insight Jesus demonstrated. All it takes is for you to do what Jesus did in order to see what Jesus saw. This requires involvement, understanding, prayer, and action.

Involvement

Involvement takes place when you and I move outside the church walls and meet people on their turf. Sometimes we don't have to say a thing; just being there says it all. When someone is hurting badly and you can't really do anything, just sitting with him or her or being with them is often enough. The power of presence goes a long way.

Jean Cullen, who is on staff with Woman's Missionary Union® (WMU®), told me that she learned the power of presence by observing a member of her Sunday School class in his ministry to the homeless. As the class members served food in a soup kitchen, Jean noticed a man wearing layers of clothing and a coat that was too big for him. His long hair was dirty and matted. He was graciously thanking those serving as he went through the line when her classmate called him by name. The church member had served there often, and had begun developing a relationship with this man. Later, Jean said, she saw the two of them sitting at the table, eating together and talking meaningfully.

> Suddenly the man was no longer one of the "regulars." He was a man who had parents, family, a history. He was a man who could, in that moment, have a relationship with the man in our class. Standing there, watching the exchange, I was struck by the power of presence. The man from our class wasn't offering a job or money or anything. He was just there, listening and talking. He was present, which reminded me of what Christ did for us.

Jesus got His perspective the same way—through involvement. He saw people's needs because He was out among them. He was involved in their lives. He went to their parties, weddings, and funerals. He attended synagogue and temple observances with them, and was a frequent guest at dinner gatherings. He had conversations with sick people, wept with grieving people, and bantered with two of His favorite women—His mother and Martha. He discussed theology with the Sadducees and Pharisees, law with the politicians and attorneys, and the kingdom of heaven with anybody who would listen. He also talked about farming, commerce, finances, and family life. He went fishing, rode in parades, and camped out with 12 rowdy men. He cooked a meal at least once, frequently played with children, and took the time to visit with Peter's mother-in-law. Jesus never had a problem knowing what people's needs were; He stayed engaged in their lives enough to see. Jean Cullen comments:

> God could have provided salvation for us through any means. But God chose to become present with us—to become one of us. The fact that we are saved through a *relationship* with Christ demonstrates the power of relationship in our lives, relationship with those who are near us every day and relationship with those far removed from us.

If you limit your "ministry" to what you can accomplish in a one-hour time slot on Sunday, you'll never develop love eyes. It takes involvement in the lives of other people. Love eyes are developed in the Little League stands, in the marketplace, and in the homes (or homeless shelters) of other people. Engage! And as you do, watch. Ask God to help you see what He sees.

Understanding

Refocusing your love eyes always requires taking the time to understand the people we are in relationship with. Glynnis Whitwer, author and speaker, reminds us that this is particularly important in an environment in which people seem to have it all together—particularly in our church gatherings.

> Look around you at any church service and you'll see normal looking people. Their lives must be great, you think. They walk in with a smile and out with a smile. All the while, many of them are dying by increments on the inside. Despair, fear, anger, questions. Is this all there is? Does anybody care? Will someone love ME?
>
> Our churches are filled with hurting people, carelessly tossed aside by someone during the week. Their hearts and minds reverberate with echoes of angry words spoken to them and unkind actions done to them. They walk into

our churches and small groups with a filament of hope and a last-ditch prayer. What will they find?

Jesus took the time to meet and understand those who were "dying by increments on the inside." He met them at their point of need. Studied them. Searched them. Listened to them. And what He saw broke His heart. It will move your heart too. But first, you will have to confront any tendency to make rash judgments about people who are different.

Refocusing our love eyes happens when we pray.

Jean Cullen discovered that the hard way when she went to a shelter for women and children to interview a woman who had agreed to meet with her. This mother of two was single and struggling to get back on her feet. Jean braced herself for a story about an abusive relationship, or perhaps how the woman had abused drugs or alcohol. Little did she realize how wrong her assumptions had been. This woman was an English teacher with a master's degree. She had divorced and then was laid off during cutbacks. Without financial resources or personal support, she found herself in a temporary housing program.

> I found that while we spent time on my questions, our conversation really became about her fears, how her circumstances were affecting her children, her shame, embarrassment, and loneliness. I couldn't give her anything, and I couldn't offer her a job. But I was present with her for two hours. Now the mother of two children of my own, I look back and realize that, in that moment, the woman I talked with that day simply needed someone to be present with her. She wanted someone to know her, not just her needs.

This takes time. It takes two-way conversation. It requires that we see beneath the surface of the plastic smiles and stop what we're doing to show people honor and respect. That was Jesus' secret. Glynnis Whitwer comments:

It wasn't Jesus' well-manicured conversations that did it; He didn't seem to be a master of small talk. Reading about Jesus' interactions with people, we find He got to the heart of the matter very quickly. Jesus' compassion must have radiated from Him because it didn't take long for people to open their pain-filled hearts. When they did, Jesus introduced God's healing love.

Prayer

Refocusing our love eyes happens when we *pray* diligently for others. Jesus's perspective came from the fact that He interceded for people faithfully. His intimacy with the Father led to vision from the Father. The same is true for you and me. Loving as Jesus loves has to begin by being intimate with Him. Time spent in prayer and in His Word will, indeed, help us to love as He loves. By letting Him be a part of everything we do, say, or think daily, we are able to see those around us who are hurting and truly in need. Only then can we love others like He wants us to love. If we pretend to be intimate and try to do things in our own power, not in His, we won't enter into the great joy or experience the perspective that comes from authentic intimacy with Christ.

Intimacy with Jesus should be natural for us believers, but it isn't. We often don't give Him enough time. We don't make Him a part of every minute of every day in all that we do. However, we will see the difference it makes when we try spending time with the Lord *before* we arrive at church. We will see how it makes a difference in what we see when we actually get there. We can also consistently commune with the Lord before going into the marketplace, and we will receive in a fresh way the ability to see as He sees, hear as He hears, talk as He talks, and touch as He would touch, and reach out. Without that intimacy with the Father, we can't begin to love as He loves.

When we think about the people the Lord has brought into our lives and how much we love them (or don't), and pray daily that the Lord will show us how to love the way that Jesus loves, we won't say the same old "whatever" prayer—"Lord, if there is anything I can do, just let me know." We will go beyond that and get specific. As we continue to pray, we can ask Him to show us *who* it is that He has for us to show His love today. Who is in need around us? We can ask Him to open our eyes and help us see through the love eyes of Jesus.

Important as private prayer is, intimacy with the Lord isn't limited to our "closet" time (Matthew 6:6). Jesus was stirred to pray as He interacted with people. We should be too. What about the person who checks us out of the grocery store or waits on us at a restaurant? When our eyes are open, ears are ready to hear, and we are ready to reach out in the love of Jesus, He will actually show us how to pray for others. Then we can really know how to minister to and love them in His name. I have been a witness to many other individuals and missionaries who have yielded themselves to be vessels for God's love: Dr. Joanne Goatcher, a missionary pediatrician in Thailand, daily ministered to families whose children needed not only physical attention but spiritual help as well. Betty Butcher, who worked alongside her husband, Dr. Orby Butcher, poured out herself to women who lived in poverty while helping them through Thai Country Trim—today WorldCrafts—find a way to feed their children and to find their way to Jesus. Gayla Parker, a missionary to the Philippines, poured out herself daily to the women who lived in such fear and darkness. These are just a few examples of God's call—for us to love in action. My dad was a great example to me—of being intimate with the Father, even while in motion.

Action

When our eyes are open *and* our hands are willing, *and* our feet are moving toward the needs of others, an amazing thing happens— our ability to see from Christ's perspective becomes even sharper. We look around ourselves with new eyes—His eyes! Then we reach out to others with His touch and are amazed at the many avenues through which we can love. We will be compelled to love others because we love Him first.

What we believe shows up in how we act. As we grow in our confidence that the Lord loves us completely, as we respond to Him in intimate worship and praise, and as we stay filled and controlled by the Holy Spirit, His love will overflow into the lives of people around us. I don't think this is exceptional—I think this is God's normal expectation of His children. He expects us to love like Jesus loved. Jesus told the disciples that they would be known by the way they treated and loved others. The same is true about us—others will know how much we love Him by our actions.

So often it seems as though we talk about loving like Jesus, but we simply don't put it into action. It's easy to allow distractions, personal concerns, or the opinions of others to get in the way of loving like Jesus would love. We need to act out of the love in our hearts because of who we trust. If our hearts trust the Lord, then His love will flow out of us and take root in others through our decisive action.

Jesus gave us some specific ways to show our love in Matthew 25:35–36. These ways get us started!

> For I was hungry
> and you gave Me something to eat;
> I was thirsty
> and you gave Me something to drink;
> I was a stranger and you took Me in;
> I was naked and you clothed Me;
> I was sick and you took care of Me;
> I was in prison and you visited Me.
> —Matthew 25:35–36

Feeding the hungry, giving water to the thirsty, helping strangers, clothing the naked, caring for the sick, and visiting prisoners— these are all practical action steps that both *express* and *generate* our ability to see deeply into the hearts and needs of others. We can't do these types of things without having love eyes. But we also can't refocus our love eyes without doing these types of things.

God's Word says, "Little children, we must not love in word or speech, but in deed and truth" (1 John 3:18). I can't simply say I love people. I must show them this love by my actions. As I do, I can't help but see even more clearly from God's perspective.

One of the most revealing tests of our love is found in our willingness to take action in expressing love to those who are different. How well do we use our love eyes to act in love toward those who live differently, with different customs, smells, economic levels, dress, and values? What about our enemies? Acting in love toward them is impossible to do without Jesus's love eyes. Missions workers in foreign places often are called to love people groups that are out to kill or to destroy them. How do they see people like that with love? Only by looking at them through Jesus's love eyes.

How do we love a group whose dress disturbs us—whose tattoos and piercings say loudly that they're different? Or whose actions declare that they expect to be rejected? We have to see them with love eyes—to see them as Jesus would. How do we love the homeless, who have no place to eat, to bathe, to live, except the street? We have to look at them with love eyes—as Jesus would see them and love them as He would love them.

Love eyes are anything but blind.

Gary Thomas, in *The Beautiful Fight*, describes an experience he had with the Lord that was similar to that of Jesus seeing the multitudes. As he walked through Terminal F of Chicago's O'Hare Airport, he saw people doing the typical things busy travelers do: typing on laptops, waiting in lines, or getting something to eat. Then, he says, almost as though a shadow passed over them, he seemed to be able to see them as God does. They were real individuals with real concerns, and God's heart was beating for every one of them.

> At that moment, the "F" terminal of the Chicago airport suddenly morphed into a sanctuary, a holy place of possibility. I didn't see job titles, expensive jewelry, business success, or power. I just saw people—some alienated from God, others knowing him but not relating to him much, still others actively open to hearing his voice. What I saw were just *people,* without all the trappings— and what defined them beyond anything else was how they relate (or don't relate) to God.

By a gracious act of God, Gary saw what Jesus saw on a different day, in a different age and place. But their experience can also be ours. "True Christian eyesight," Gary Thomas says, in *The Beautiful Fight*, "is about seeing others with the eyes of God—

noticing the unnoticed, not being distracted by what the world considers important, caring about those we once would have gladly looked past." Unlike the way I laugh off my husband's compliments sometimes, or the ways my children speak of love eyes as if they're naive, true love *sees*, and sees clearly. Love eyes are anything but blind. To see what God sees is to engage with those He cares about, to seek to understand them deeply, to pray for them fervently, and to serve them faithfully. *Feeling* that love is nice; *seeing* the need and God's heart toward people, however, is absolutely necessary.

You can't love without it.

For Reflection and Discussion

1. Write about a time when you, one of your children, or someone else needed some "love eyes, please." Perhaps something that's funny now, but not too funny back then.

2. What are some of the ways Jesus involved Himself in the everyday lives of people, both publicly and privately, as recorded in John, chapter 2?

3. In Matthew 20:29–34, what did Jesus do to more fully understand the needs of these two men?

4. What was the relationship between prayer and Paul's direction for ministry as shown in Acts 16:6–10?

5. How has God taught us to show love to people who are different in some way? What makes it difficult, and how does God give us His "love eyes" perspective?

Chapter 4

Listening with His Ears

L ove listens, and first love listens from the heart. Jesus
demonstrated an amazing ability to love others by hearing
past their words and identifying the content of their hearts.
He now calls us to do the same. And sometimes He sends a
flesh-and-blood reminder of what He's talking about. Sompon
was mine.

Sompon was a young Thai girl in Little Rock, Arkansas, who
phoned to ask if I would teach her English. I agreed. We needed
to meet somewhere she could find, so we met at our church. Being
a large church, I figured she could find it easily. We met and had
our lesson, and I was anxious to get on with my next ministry
task. To be honest, I was a bit proud of myself, thinking I had
done my "good deed for the day." (I had even taught English
from the New Testament!)

Sompon wasn't ready to leave. She asked, "Why do you
build such a big temple instead of helping those who need help
around you?"

In spite of my temptation to hurry away, I had to stop and regroup. Her question forced me to listen to understand truly what she was saying. When I did, I realized that she had virtually nothing. She was in the United States trying to make a life for herself and to send money back home. But she had virtually no material possessions. She knew no one. She had very little money or food, no transportation, and no medical care. Moreover, she had no hope because she didn't know Jesus as Savior. The Lord opened my heart by opening my ears and enabling me to hear her with *His* ears and heart.

We start by learning to listen to God!

Over the next month, Sompon and I met each week to learn English. However, our relationship went much deeper. We spent time together shopping. We ate together. And through cultivating a relationship based on listening and understanding, I was able to share the love of Christ with this amazing girl. Sompon came to know the Lord and her whole life changed. She is now a bold, living witness to her Buddhist family across the globe in Thailand. And I was reminded of an important lesson. Love listens! By simply listening to someone with love and concern, we can literally have an impact in the world!

Peter Lord, in his book *Hearing God*, tells of an experience he had that illustrates the relationship between love and hearing. During a wedding reception at his home, he stepped outside for a moment to take a break from the crowd. There he discovered one of the ushers from the wedding standing on the small path leading from the front door to the driveway. His head was cocked, and he was peering intently at the plants beside the walk.

"Mr. Lord," he said in awe, "do you know that you have 18 different kinds of crickets in those bushes?"

Crickets? Peter stared at him blankly. He had lived there for years and had never consciously heard a single cricket! But this young man was a graduate student in entomology at the University of Florida, and had learned to distinguish more than 200 different types of cricket calls with his natural ear.

To one man, crickets were a noisy insect. To another, they were the object of great interest and love. One ignored them; the other listened with a desire to understand. And the more the graduate student listened and studied, the more he loved the object of his search and understanding.

This chapter isn't about the *mechanics* of listening so much as it is about the *relationships* involved in listening. I believe this was one of the secrets of the amazing ability of Jesus to understand the hearts of the people to whom He ministered. Jesus described His ministry by saying, "The words I speak to you I do not speak on My own. The Father who lives in Me does His works" (John 14:10). His intimacy with the Father was the basis for His understanding of people. The same goes for us today. If we want to love by listening, we start by learning to listen to God! Only then can we perceive the heart needs of the people we encounter, in order to express genuine love to them.

Hearing God's Voice

I have a new computer, and it has ears, so to speak. It's made to respond to verbal commands and words. Voice recognition, it's called. Just one problem—I can't seem to get it to recognize my accent! The good news is that the engineers who designed this technology made it possible to train the computer software to recognize the voice of its owner. Our Designer did the same thing when He created us. Of course, I am not talking about hearing a human voice as the audible voice of God; He created us with the ability to be trained to recognize His voice in our spirit. Do *you* recognize God's voice when He speaks to you through prayer, through His Word, through other Christians, through His divine orchestration of circumstances? Has He "spoken" to you lately?

Sometimes God's voice is still and quiet. Many times I wonder if I have heard Him in my thoughts. At other times, God's voice is loud and strong and I have no doubt that He's talking to *me*! Once I was on a plane going to California. It was a long trip, and we'd gone a long way already. The lights on the plane dimmed, and it was quiet. The reading lights beamed above some people's heads, and in other seats people were asleep. I had been working on a talk and praying, and the Lord spoke to me! It was so clear and seemed so loud in my heart and mind that, for an instant, I thought I could literally hear His voice in my ears! I even looked around. Yes, everyone was asleep. God was communicating clearly and definitively to my mind and heart.

This is not strange or superstitious. Jesus Himself compared our relationship to Him as that of sheep to a shepherd. "My sheep hear My voice," He said. "I know them, and they follow Me. I give them eternal life, and they will never perish—ever! No one will snatch them out of My hand" (John 10:27–28). Sheep know their shepherd's literal voice. They come when he calls because they have learned to trust him. Shepherds spend time with the sheep and each grows in the knowledge of the other.

We learn to recognize God's spiritual voice in the same way. We have to spend time with Him so we can learn to recognize *His* voice and discern it from our *own*, or from the voice of the enemy. Gary Thomas expresses his view in *The Beautiful Fight*:

> "God's voice has a certain style and tone that mark it as genuine. Just as those who catch counterfeit money makers train by becoming obsessively familiar with the real thing, so we build walls between ourselves and deception by patiently, perseveringly, and faithfully, over time, practicing the presence of God."

Abraham knew God's audible voice. The Book of Genesis describes scene after scene in which Abraham, through time spent listening to God, heard the literal voice of the Lord—making promises, giving commands, and encouraging faith. Abraham seemed to be in constant communication with God. The more he prayed and listened, the greater his love and trust in God. Only such a love and faith could pass Abraham's ultimate test of offering his long-awaited son, Isaac, as a sacrifice to God (Genesis 22). Little did he know that this act of not withholding his only son would foreshadow the ultimate act of sacrificial love by God Himself. Abraham was becoming more and more like the God he loved because he listened to God's voice.

Heeding God's Direction

When God communicates, it is often in the form of guiding His people through steps of obedience or direction. He loves us enough to lead us and include us in His plan. But to experience the fullness of that plan, we have to let go of our own plans.

Even as a child, before I trusted Christ as my Savior, I had a plan. I would be a doctor, a missionary in Thailand working in the Bangkla Baptist Hospital. I had worked, from the age of seven, alongside my dad while he operated, and that was all I needed to know. I was ready! That was *my* plan, however admirable and noble. When I became a believer, I began to discover that God had His own direction for my life.

Being called is still one of the great mysteries of the Christian life.

In chapter 1, I mentioned my parents and their sense of being called by God to the missions field. Being called is still one of the great mysteries of the Christian life. But for everyone who has that personal, intimate relationship with Jesus Christ, He has started them on a journey with Him the moment they said yes to His invitation! Yes, challenges, questions, and roadblocks are sometimes part of that journey, but we have a special Guide—the Author and Finisher of our faith (Hebrews 12:2).

What do we think about when we hear the word *journey*? I think about what I need that will get me where I am going! A map or a GPS system is certainly helpful, but only if I use them, of course. When some people drive, they say that they don't need a map to get to their destination. However, sometimes they don't get to where they are going, or they're late.

Now a GPS system is another story. My husband, Mark, says these things are the greatest invention since golf—quite a compliment if you knew him. We turn that box on and it says, "Calculating . . . calculating." Then it gives us the right directions— people's directions, that is, to get to our destination. If we miss the directions for some reason, the GPS will say, "Recalculating . . . recalculating," and then spit out a new set of instructions. These systems were obviously built by people with the bottom line in mind. When giving directions, they say something like, "Go north 3.5 miles and then turn east." If I had designed GPS systems, I would say something like, "Go to the drugstore on the right and then left and go past the green house and turn at the red maple tree."

Airline pilots do the same thing. The safety and success of every flight depend on the ability of pilots to communicate with the tower and follow instructions. On some of the landings I have endured, in stormy or severely windy conditions, I certainly *prayed* that the pilot was talking to the tower!

Don't you wish we had a GPS system for finding God's will, or a compass? Author Travis Collins uses that metaphor in his book *Directionally Challenged: How to Find and Follow God's Course for Your Life.* Wouldn't it be great to always know where God wants us to go and always know what He wants us to do? God does promise us this. "And whenever you turn to the right or to the left, your ears will hear this command behind you: 'This is the way. Walk in it'" (Isaiah 30:21). We don't have a GPS around our necks telling us, "Recalculating . . . recalculating" when we get off track. But we do have God's Word and God's Spirit to guide us each step of this journey.

Even the Apostle Paul experienced the need to "recalculate." As he and his missionary team went through the region of Phrygia and Galatia, they were prevented by the Holy Spirit from speaking the gospel in the province of Asia. So they tried to go to Bithynia, but the Spirit of Jesus did not allow them to go there either. So they bypassed Mysia and went to Troas. There, during the night, Paul had a vision in which he saw a Macedonian man pleading with him, "Cross over to Macedonia and help us!" (Acts 16:9). Writing about this experience, Luke says that "after he had seen the vision, we immediately made efforts to set out for Macedonia, concluding that God had called us to evangelize them" (Acts 16:10).

Heeding God's direction also means that when God communicates, we don't "recalculate" on our own. That was certainly true in Abraham's case. When told to take his only son, Isaac, and offer him as a burnt offering to the Lord, Abraham didn't argue. He didn't refuse. He didn't say, "I don't want to do this." He was obedient to God's direction, and the Lord honored him.

Love Has a Middle Name

God didn't have to use Abraham's middle name (whatever that was). But sometimes His love will, if necessary. My youngest child is a boy—John Mark Miller. I called him by his middle name so often when he was in trouble that several of us call him by that to this day!

When you were a child, were you ever playing outside when you heard your mom call you to come inside—with a tone that told you exactly what was coming next? Or maybe you call your children with a certain tone when you want them to come in *now*! You want to make sure that they hear you first of all, then you want to make sure that they understand what you mean by that call and that they do what you call them to do! I remember vividly my mom calling me one afternoon and I knew by the tone that I was in trouble any way I looked at it! Did I answer and get into trouble or did I pretend that I didn't hear her and hope that it would help? You know what I am talking about!

I have to be still to perceive God's voice.

Do you feel as though God uses your middle name to get your attention? To this day, my mother *still* uses my middle name when she wants my attention. Have you ever heard the Lord call you, and didn't want to answer Him because you knew what was next if you did? Hearing the Lord call us is often hard because we are too busy to listen, or we are too focused on ourselves or our children or what is going on around us. Sometimes we even might miss the Lord prompting us because we are too busy "doing" for the Lord.

I have to be still to perceive God's voice. Life gets so busy sometimes that it's hard to grasp His guidance above the roar of my daily life, so I am committed to be very intentional about taking the time to pray and to read His Word. I have to listen daily to what He is showing me. For whatever reason, the Lord often impresses me while I am flying on airplanes—especially at night when it is quiet and I view His incredible creation from the airplane window. One such time, I didn't want to listen. God impressed me with the thought of being national WMU president. My mind responded that He couldn't have possibly said I was to do this! I wasn't going to listen to His call to do that. In fact, He had to confirm this call to me several times before I *knew* this was what He wanted me to do. When I said yes, I began to receive His confirmation in many ways. And I learned to listen to the people that I love—and the people He loves—in a deeper way too.

Understanding Your Neighbor

Learning to discern God's voice makes it possible for us to listen to and understand people's hearts. Just as loving one's neighbor follows loving God (Matthew 22:37–40), so listening to the heart of a neighbor follows listening to the heart of the Lord. Jesus illustrated this in a remarkable way the night before His betrayal. He said to Peter, "Simon, Simon, look out! Satan has asked to sift you like wheat. But I have prayed for you, that your faith may not fail. And you, when you have turned back, strengthen your brothers" (Luke 22:31–32). By knowing His Father's voice, and praying for Peter, Jesus understood something of this disciple's heart—even some things Peter didn't understand about himself. And Peter wasn't pleased with what he was hearing.

"Lord, he told Him, 'I'm ready to go with You both to prison and to death!'"

"I tell you, Peter," He said, "the rooster will not crow today until you deny three times that you know Me!" (Luke 22:33–34).

It's easy in our relationships to hear the people's words without actually hearing their hearts. It's humbling to think how many times I may have passed someone—even at church—and asked how he or she was without really waiting for an answer. I didn't truly look at them, or stop and ask, "What's going on in your life?" People all around us are hurting and we have to stop and *listen* to them and *hear* them, as Jesus would.

An experiment conducted at Princeton Seminary ("From Jerusalem to Jericho: A Study of Situational and Dispositional Variables in Helping Behavior") illustrates the point. It was designed to test people's natural impulse to be good to others—the altruistic impulse. A cohort of students in a room prepared for a sermon on which they would be graded. Half were preaching from the parable of the good Samaritan; the other half on anything they chose. The experiment was to see what they would do if they were on their way to preach and passed a man who apparently was hurt. Would they stop *and* help him?

Generally speaking, most of the students failed to stop. Even those preparing to preach on the good Samaritan didn't do better than the others. The only hopeful variable was time. Of those who were told they were running late, only one in ten stopped to help the man. Yet those who knew they had plenty of time stopped to help, at a rate of 60 percent.

The implications of this research are astonishing. It suggests that when we *make* time and believe we *have* time to focus on others' needs, we are far more likely to do so. Being in a hurry, on the other hand, narrows our focus. Hurriedness can completely shut out someone who is in obvious pain and standing right next to us. We often talk about "taking the time" and "understanding the heart." The truth is that we can't take the time or understand the heart of someone whose voice we're oblivious to hearing. And we pass people without hearing them on a daily basis, don't we?

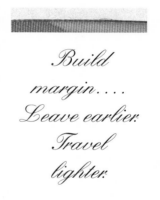

Build margin. . . . Leave earlier. Travel lighter.

So how do we change that? It starts by making the time, first with God, then with others. That's what Richard Swenson's brilliant book *Margin* is all about. By not crowding every waking moment with noise and tasks to be done, by not spending every available dollar, and by not draining every ounce of our emotional and physical energy, we are then free to notice, to hear, to listen to the heart, to *understand,* to *love.* Build margin, and we will improve our ability to hear and serve the people around us. Leave earlier. Travel lighter. Spend some time listening, or simply observing people. And we will be more available, happier, and more effective at showing Christ's love.

Taking the time to understand the heart has taught me to love others, even when I haven't felt like loving them—can't love them. I have learned to love others when they have made me upset and angry. How loving do we feel, for example, when we're dealing with others who lash out in anger and say things they don't mean? Those are the times when, by hearing God's voice and resting in His grace, we must listen beyond that anger. We need to listen as the Lord would to what is *really* going on—to why they are angry and are lashing out in the first place.

The Language of the Heart

Jesus listened to people with first-love concern. In situation after situation, He listened to the hearts, not just the words of people. When Nicodemus offered Him flattering words, Jesus heard the heart of one who was searching for life (John 3:1–21). When the woman at the well arrived at midday to draw water, Jesus saw the heart of a local moral reject, seeking to avoid public scrutiny and scorn (John 4:7–30). When Andrew and Philip asked to see where He was staying, Jesus heard in their question a desire for relationship and mentoring (John 1:38). When Simon Peter humbled himself before Jesus after his miraculous catch of fish, Jesus heard in his words the incredible potential to be a fisher of men (Luke 5:10). In these and many other situations, Jesus acknowledged their words, but listened intently to discover their *hearts*. He understood what we must—that words sometimes reveal the heart, and at other times they conceal it.

Listening . . . it's a gift that we give.

The heart speaks a language of its own—a language of desires and feelings, relationships and dreams, time and eternity. And we are all made for hearts to connect. So how did and does Jesus understand the heart's language? By listening and loving with His own heart. Discernment is the by-product of love. When our children, for example, pour out their hearts to us about school or friends, what they may really be telling us is how lonely they are, or how depressed and confused they are. When co-workers tell us about last night's party or joke about someone else in the workplace, they may be masking their own loneliness. We have the capacity to reach beyond the external language and listen as the Lord would have us to do—to love them with His ears. Sometimes they just want us to hear them!

For Jesus, sometimes even His speaking was an act of listening. Through speaking the language of love, He was saying to others, "I hear your heart; I understand you!" When He invited Himself to lunch with Zacchaeus (Luke 19:1–10), He saw a despised man who was ready to change his life. When He called Peter and Andrew, James and John, He spoke to the hearts of men who wanted their lives to count for more than making a living (Matthew 4:19–22). When He asked the Samaritan woman to go call her husband, He spoke to the heart of someone who desperately wanted to be loved and accepted (John 4:16–18). We, too, can speak to others in a way that shows we understand—or are trying to understand—their hearts.

It has been said that listening isn't only a need that we have— it's a gift that we give. When we listen to the voice of the Lord, we are offering Him the gift of worship and fellowship. When we listen to our neighbors as the Lord first listens to us, we offer them the gift of life, connection, affirmation, and encouragement. When we slow down long enough to "be still and know He is God" (Psalm 46:10), or be interrupted joyfully by the needs of a stranger or friend, we are offering gifts to all three—to God, to our neighbor, and to ourselves.

Simply put, when we listen with His ear to the language of someone else's heart, we love.

Love isn't passive. It also reaches out to touch others with His hands. That's what we'll explore in the next chapter.

For Reflection and Discussion

1. What are some ways that God speaks to different people? With which of these can you most identify?

2. How did the Lord ultimately reveal Himself to Elijah in 1 Kings 19:10–14? Why did Elijah need to "recalibrate" his ability to discern God's voice?

3. Do you ever feel the need, as Paul did in Acts 16, to "recalculate" what you're hearing from the Lord? How does the Lord guide you along the way to recalculate your direction?

4. Discernment is the by-product of love. In Luke 19:1–10, what was the difference between the way Jesus approached Zacchaeus and the way other people had?

5. What are some ways the Lord has been speaking to you lately? How is He leading or encouraging you, and how are you responding?

Chapter 5

Touching with His Hands

In *The Friendship Factor*, Alan Loy McGinnis relates the story of a group of medical students, focusing on one student in particular. What made this medical student different? Why was he so especially loved by the children and greeted with joy? That's what his colleagues in the children's ward of the large eastern hospital wanted to know. So one of his group members agreed to follow him and find out what it was about him that attracted the children. The observer didn't find anything all that unusual until the young doctor made his last round at night, and the mystery was solved: he kissed every child good night.

Sometimes we make love too complicated. Expressing it can be as simple as a hand on a shoulder, a kiss on the cheek, or a hug. Jesus modeled this in His ministry. In its fellowship, the early church modeled these actions and they are still important expressions of love today. Love connects! God's love uses our feet to go where people are, and our hands to reach out, to serve, to affirm, and to comfort.

The early church's early custom was to greet one another with a "holy kiss" (Romans 16:16; 1 Corinthians 16:20; 2 Corinthians 13:12; 1 Thessalonians 5:26). Yet this is more than social custom; the need for touch begins in infancy. Infants not touched lovingly end up suffering emotional deprivation as adults. Touch relieves stress, adds to happiness, and promotes a healthy body, mind, and soul. Older people need to be touched, as well as those who are ill. In fact, experiments show that "people in deep comas often show improved heart rates when their hands are held by doctors or nurses" ("Loneliness Can Kill You," *Time*, September 5, 1977). Touching is a simple act, but one easily overlooked due to distractions and the pace of life we encounter. In failing to express love in this simplest of ways, we cheat ourselves and others, and only add to the isolation that people feel.

Touching is a simple act, but one easily overlooked.

A Biblical View of Loneliness

Psalm 88 gives a graphic picture of loneliness. Read carefully, and you will see some of the symptoms of loneliness. Read from the perspective of a starving refugee in Africa, an earthquake victim in China, a nursing home resident in your town, or others who need love's touch:

> Lord, God of my salvation,
> I cry out before You day and night.
> May my prayer reach Your presence;
> listen to my cry.
> For I have had enough troubles,
> and my life is near Sheol.
> I am counted among those going down to the Pit.
> I am like a man without strength,
> abandoned among the dead.
> I am like the slain lying in the grave,
> whom You no longer remember,
> and who are cut off from Your care.

You have put me in the lowest part of the Pit,
in the darkest places, in the depths.
Your wrath weighs heavily on me;
You have overwhelmed me with all Your waves. Selah.
You have distanced my friends from me;
You have made me repulsive to them.
I am shut in and cannot go out.
My eyes are worn out from crying.
Lord, I cry out to You all day long;
I spread out my hands to You.
Do You work wonders for the dead?
Do departed spirits rise up to praise You? Selah.
Will Your faithful love be declared in the grave,
Your faithfulness in Abaddon?
Will Your wonders be known in the darkness,
or Your righteousness in the land of oblivion?
But I call to You for help, Lord;
in the morning my prayer meets You.
Lord, why do You reject me?
Why do You hide Your face from me?
From my youth, I have been afflicted and near death.
I suffer Your horrors; I am desperate.
Your wrath sweeps over me;
Your terrors destroy me.
They surround me like water all day long;
they close in on me from every side.
You have distanced loved one and neighbor from me;
darkness is my only friend.
—Psalm 88

Lonely people, if they have prayed at all, feel God has not heard their prayer, or has deserted them. Many have reached emotional and physical limits, and feel they can't take anymore. Some think they may as well be dead. They feel forgotten and passed by. This happens often to people who were once the center of attention or activity and who, for whatever reason, aren't anymore.

Lonely people feel separated from their friends. Relocation, death, or some other change in circumstances often creates a barrier between them and those they love. They may feel untouchable.

They can be self-conscious and, as the psalmist wrote, may feel "repulsive." I have noticed that many lonely people desperately long to have a hand held, or for someone to hug them or put their arm around them. Loneliness is often the result of not being able to get out. This may apply to sick or elderly people, or to parents of sick or disabled children. Often those who *would* do something about their loneliness are unable to do so. As a result, many lonely people end up focusing their minds on death, living in great fear while feeling defenseless and helpless. They need to experience God's security and peace. This is where we enter. Love calls us to connect—to touch the untouchable and reach out tangibly to those in greatest need.

Jesus did and said so many profound and miraculous things during His earthly ministry that it's easy to overlook one of His most distinguishing attributes: *Jesus touched people*. He touched infants and small children whom the disciples wanted no part in reaching. Terrified disciples on stormy seas and frightening mountaintops, reassuring them of His love and care. He touched the unclean—spiritual and social rejects who desperately needed a new beginning. The sick, whose bodies were ravaged with fever or were incapacitated by lifelong or terminal afflictions. He touched the captives, who were prisoners of spiritual darkness and bondage, and set them free. And in a generation in which the spiritual haves never really connected with the have-nots, Jesus transformed those people by going where they were, and touching their lives and bodies with kindness and healing. Now He sends us to do the same (John 20:21).

The Connecting Touch

We moved to Bangkla after my dad had passed the Thai medical boards. This village had no medical care, had hardly even seen a foreigner, had no cars—and here comes this US family with a dog and three young girls. We watched, as did the villagers, as the beautiful hospital was built. And then the time came to train the first class of nurses and nurse aides. My sisters and I thought that it would be fun to get to see what our new Thai friends were being taught. Little did we know that they were going to practice on us! I remember lying on bed after bed while they changed the sheets as they practiced making a bed with someone in it. We were wrapped up and bandaged up—thank goodness we weren't stuck with needles! But even in something as formal as training or as fun as being a child volunteer, we connected. We were able to reach across a completely foreign language and culture barrier and build relationships in the name of Christ.

I saw miracles happen. I also saw heartbreaking things happen.

Even as a child, I knew that one of the best ways to tell people about Jesus was through meeting a physical need. Through the daily passion and commitment of my parents, I saw miracles happen. I also saw heartbreaking things happen—like the man whose arm had been severed. He walked for over four days, carrying his arm in brown paper, hoping that the great US doctor could help him. His arm couldn't be saved, but he heard about how *he* could be saved—and he was.

Word spread really quickly about the medical care at the hospital. People often walked for days to come and be seen by one of the doctors in Bangkla. I often helped as doctors saw patients—and not one person went through the hospital without hearing about Jesus Christ from one of the missionaries. Passionate about health care, passionate about sharing Jesus, passionate about *connecting* with people who were unnoticed or forgotten—that's what I saw every day growing up.

Not every effort to connect landed in the way it was intended. My father had to preach at church one Sunday morning—something he usually didn't do. He was preaching on the Cross and Christ's love. The problem was that in Thai, which is a tonal language, the words for cross and pants are very similar, depending on tone. That Sunday morning, to a whole congregation that needed to hear about Jesus and the Cross, Daddy preached on the pants of Christ! They knew what he was saying; they laughed as he preached, and he didn't know why. And he certainly didn't think that the Cross was something to laugh about. However, his preaching caused them to listen closely and several came to know the Lord that day—as they heard about the "pants"!

We tried to find ways that we could help.

That brings up an important point. Sometimes we isolate or withdraw from others because we are anxious about not doing everything correctly. Yet God is looking for our willingness and availability, and will honor even a flawed expression of love offered with a humble and caring heart. Because Daddy had already touched lives by connecting with them medically, the precious Thai people were willing to overlook his mistakes and recognize the love and truth behind his message.

The Blessing Touch

First-century Jewish parents had a tradition of asking a rabbi to bless their children. It's not surprising that parents would bring their infants and small children to Jesus for the same reason. Thinking they were doing Jesus a favor, the disciples told the parents that what they were doing was wrong, and to stop it. Jesus intervened with some public rebuking of His own! "Let the little children come to Me. Don't stop them, for the kingdom of God belongs to such as these. I assure you: Whoever does not welcome the kingdom of God like a little child will never enter it" (Mark 10:14–15).

Mark then records that Jesus took these children in His arms, laid His hands on them, and blessed them. In doing so, Jesus was being much more than ceremonial. He was a catalyst of God's favor and blessing upon the lives of some special people who were probably too young to understand what was happening. The word for blessed occurs only here in the New Testament and means to eulogize emphatically. Jesus was excited, passionate, and knew that "life and death are in the power of the tongue" (Proverbs 18:21). He spoke words conveying God's blessing over each one, individually. All the while, He was holding them or laying His hands on them. This symbolized setting someone apart for service, conveying something from one person to another, or authorizing someone to represent the individual or group. Such an act by Jesus conveyed a very important message to both the parents and to the children: *You are loved and you are important to the kingdom.*

As missionary kids, we believed we had a calling to teach others about Jesus as much as our parents did. So we tried to find ways that we could help. One thing we noticed was that the children at the orphanage were not thriving because they were not being held. It was easy to tell the difference between the babies that had been held often and those that hadn't. We used to go to the orphanage to rock and hold babies as often as we could. As teenagers, we saw it as something small we could do. Looking back on it now, I believe such simple expressions of love and care had a more profound impact than we realized at the time. To hold a baby is one thing; to do so in the name of Jesus Christ conveys an entirely new meaning—and a blessing.

Again, this touch of blessing isn't limited to children, and it isn't just spoken. Sometimes it is more utilitarian. After the hospital and leper clinic/home were completed and word spread about them, leprosy victims began to come from miles away. Due to the condition of the lepers' feet, most of them could not walk or run to the home. Some scooted along the road to the home, but one young man just sat on the edge of town, unable to make the journey. My dad heard about him, went out and picked the leper up, and carried him to the clinic. He was a catalyst—a conduit of God's blessing and love, expressed in a physical way.

The Reassuring Touch

Terrified! That's how Peter, James, and John felt after they were rebuked publicly by God on the Mount of Transfiguration (Matthew 17:1–8). Having seen Jesus transfigured, and Moses and Elijah's appearance as they talked with Jesus, Peter offered them a bit of Israeli first-century hospitality. "Lord, it's good for us to be here! If You want, I will make three tabernacles here: one for You, one for Moses, and one for Elijah."

While he was still speaking, God interrupted him and frightened him speechless. A bright cloud covered them, and a voice emerged from the cloud: "This is My beloved Son. I take delight in Him. Listen to Him!" (Matthew 17:5). No wonder they were terrified. Peter was used to getting himself into trouble with his impulsive speaking, but this was too much! He and his companions fell facedown and dared not move, speak, or even look up.

Then came the touch.

Again, in a simple act that's easily overlooked, Jesus came up and touched them. "Get up; don't be afraid" (Matthew 17:7). Jesus understood His disciples needed reassurance. His touch provided it.

I understand those extreme feelings of terror and reassurance. In my case, they didn't come from a thundering cloud on a mountaintop; they came from a snake in the mud! It was the end of the rainy season. It had been raining for months, but finally it was coming to a halt! The water was receding, and it was leaving a layer of mud in its wake. This was nothing new, but we never really got used to this mud. Having been cooped up in the house for so long, we were excited to finally be able to get out and go downstairs. The houses were built on stilts and the mud was under the house as we went outside. We had to watch where we stepped, but it was wonderful to be out of the house and free!

As my sister and I stepped off the last step into the mud, we found it was deeper than we had thought. Just as I lifted my foot out, a snake lunged at it, and bit my ankle. Now, I hate snakes, and the fact that it was hanging on my leg was almost more than I could take. I kept shaking my foot, but it wouldn't come off. My dad and the man who helped us with our yard cut off its body and left the head hooked to my ankle. They took me to the Bangkla Hospital, which was not far. Luckily, snake venom antidote was made in Thailand and all was taken care of with my foot. I don't remember a lot about that time, but I do remember my dad's touch. I recall being so scared about the snake as well as the bite, but his calming voice and touch helped calm me down. I knew his voice and touch, and it reassured me when I desperately needed it.

Opportunities abound to touch others with the reassuring love of Jesus. We can be the Father's touch in a sometimes frightening world. It helps to know that I don't have to be all-knowing like Jesus in order to *love* like Jesus. Sometimes people avoid reaching out to reassure others because they're afraid of saying or doing the wrong thing. But what you say with your actions will always speak louder than what you say with your answers.

The Cleansing Touch
"Lord, if You are willing, You can make me clean," the leper said

(Matthew 8:1–4). Certainly he meant the physical uncleanness of his disease and the ceremonial uncleanness that leprosy represented for any faithful Jew. But his meaning went much deeper. He also needed a heart cleansing.

"I am willing," Jesus said, "be made clean."

Did I mention that Jesus touched him?

He also was touched *by* him. Jesus, our great High Priest, is touched with the feelings of our infirmities (Hebrews 2:17–18; 4:14–15; 8:1–2). He has felt our pains, our sicknesses, and our temptations. By going where the sick were, and hanging out where the sinners were, Jesus perceived what they perceived, and felt what they felt. God's plan was more than a mail-in prescription; it was to love us on the basis of identifying and *truly knowing* us. A group of 87 teenagers and 18 adults learned that in an unforgettable way.

These kids were... starving for attention and love.

It was really hot that summer in New Orleans. The students were excited about going to the seminary to get prepped for the Vacation Bible School they would be leading in an inner-city housing project. They received their instructions and, as they listened, their faces changed from anticipation to apprehension. They would be going into an area that no one else would enter. They had to be in groups of six with an adult. They couldn't go into any building. They had to be on the bus, ready to leave the projects by 3:00—sooner, if the men came out of the houses and began to drink. I could see the fear and hesitation in their eyes. We had talked about loving kids that no one else would love, touching and meeting needs that no one else would. These kids were hungry, angry, hurting, mean, and foul-mouthed—but starving for attention and love. And this group of short-term missionaries would likely be the only expression of love they would see for a long time.

We drove into the project, and the overwhelming poverty was nearly more than we could take. The children ran toward the bus, laughing, all wanting something. The teenagers gathered together and prayed that the Lord would use their hands and hearts to help these kids. It only took seconds for the children to find a teenager and attach themselves to their sides for the rest of the day. I saw smiles as they walked hand in hand. It didn't matter that the kids' hands were filthy; they still held hands. It didn't matter that they hadn't bathed in weeks; the students still held the children in their arms. The girls let the children braid their hair—dirty hands and all. They let them have their lunches, even though they were hot and hungry. They loved and touched as the Father would. They looked beyond what they saw externally and had anticipated, and they loved unconditionally and without question. These students got out of their churches and went to be the hands of the Father.

Missions and medicine are a perfect match.

What compelled them? What kept these teens going, in the face of fear and uncertainty? A deeply felt conviction that the people they encountered were likely as dirty on the inside as on the outside. A concern that they had as real an eternal destiny as any suburban teenage or adult missionary. A confidence that Jesus Christ could do through them what no external program or tub of water could ever do. His love, poured out through the hands and hearts of an army of caring students, could change lives for eternity.

The Healing Touch

Missions and medicine are a perfect match. As physical needs are served, opportunities arise for relationships and evangelism. I was on both the giving and receiving end of that. I was in seventh grade when I first helped deliver a baby. Dad was busy elsewhere, and I was watching to see how things were progressing. Yes, my eyes widened when the baby came forth! Yes, I yelled for Dad! But what a miracle I saw!

The receiving end took place at a mission meeting. Our parents were in the town while we were out at a Baptist encampment right on the beach. Each night, we would have dinner together in the dining hall and then, after devotion, go to our bunk rooms. Little *chin-chooks* (lizards) ran all over the ceilings, eating mosquitoes; we didn't mind these. However, we had a huge lizard called a gecko, and it made noise all night. It was being really noisy and we couldn't sleep, so we decided to chase it out so we could get to bed. Using brooms and other tools, we scooted it out, but while doing that, I was bitten on the hand by a scorpion. My hand and then my arm began to get numb and I began to be truly scared. The adults there put a tourniquet on my arm and wanted to take me to a hospital, but I just wanted my dad. He met the car and treated the bite. His healing knowledge, loving touch, and instructions reassured me that all would be OK. As I have thought about that through the years, it has reminded me of my heavenly Father's love, touch, and concern that run even deeper and heal even more powerfully than a parent's.

When Jesus healed people, He used a wonderful variety of means and expressions to do so. But Matthew's description of the day Jesus healed Peter's mother-in-law of her fever carries an important reference.

> When Jesus went into Peter's house, He saw his mother-in-law lying in bed with a fever. So He touched her hand, and the fever left her. Then she got up and began to serve Him. When evening came, they brought to Him many who were demon-possessed. He drove out the spirits with a word and healed all who were sick, so that what was spoken through the prophet Isaiah might be fulfilled:
> He Himself *took our weaknesses*
> *and carried our diseases.*
> —Matthew 8:14–17 (emphasis mine)

Jesus came to do more than "fix" sick and hurting people by removing their physical problems. He came to *carry* our diseases and *take* our weaknesses. How did He do it? With His feet and hands. He *went* to where they were, and He *touched*—He engaged their diseases and weaknesses. Why is this important? *Because you love those whose lives you engage with on this level.* Yes, Jesus touched because He loved; but He also loved because He touched. Had He remained in the carpenter's shop or the synagogue, He would have limited Himself—at least on a human level.

You and I can do the same. We can carry the burdens of others (Galatians 6:2). And as we do, this fulfillment of the law of Christ is manifested in love for our brothers and sisters. There is healing power in that, of course. But we may well find that as we go where the hurting and afflicted are, *we* are the ones who experience the greater healing.

The Liberating Touch

Jesus came to set captives free. Whether it was spiritual bondage, physical bondage such as blindness or deafness, or captivity to deception, His message was clear: "If the Son sets you free, you really will be free" (John 8:36). He took on our limitations, confronted our lost condition, and overcame Satan's power to steal, kill, and destroy (John 10:10). He rescued us from the domain of darkness, established us in His kingdom, bought us back from the penalty of our sin, and forever removed the guilt of our sins (Colossians 1:13–14). The testimony of every Christ follower is that once we were lost, now we're found; once blind, but now we see.

Love did that. We are free because Jesus loves us. Now He uses us as His instruments of freedom. As in many other instances I've already described, this can be wonderfully practical. My mother demonstrated that. She was teaching a health class to the village women one morning. The women were all ears because they were hoping to help save or protect their children. One woman, who had just given birth while in the bush, had cut the umbilical cord with a bamboo stick; the baby had come down with tetanus. While the baby was fighting for his life, Mother took this opportunity to try to reach the other women of the village. They were like mothers anywhere else in the world. They wanted their children to have a chance at a better life than they had. Mother tried to show them how to cut the cord with a clean knife to prevent illness. She showed them how to bathe a baby to help it have a fighting chance at living. As she bathed that baby, I remember how she talked to the baby and gently rubbed it clean. She smiled at the baby and held it close to her chest.

These mothers hadn't seen anyone love a sick child that way, and they were soaking it all in. Mother was giving them life skills that would help their children have a chance, and break the power of disease over their infants. She didn't know how they would receive her teaching, as it went against the medicine taught in the village. But these women had seen how the US doctor was helping people who were dying, and maybe this woman was doing the same.

Mother would teach a while and then and eat with them. She ate what they gave her, often not knowing what it was she was eating! But they were grateful and were showing it by giving food and other things to her. Mother would help them laugh and feel good about themselves. Women in that culture were second-class citizens and had very few rights. Mother tried to build them up and tell them about the One who really loves them—Jesus. Buddhists are very difficult to break through to about Jesus. If they do listen, they will simply add Him to the list of gods that they already have. But Mother modeled the love that Jesus offered, and they saw a difference. She tried to demonstrate that His love would set them free from their pagan gods, limiting beliefs, and ritual behavior. She modeled ways that would help them save their children's lives, both physically and spiritually. Mother was His hands, His touch to a dark society.

To love is to touch and be touched. The more we go where the need is, and engage with those who have the need, the more love we give and receive. Jesus demonstrated that, then sent us forth to do the same.

In chapter 1, I briefly mentioned my first encounter with an HIV/AIDS patient—a smiling little two-year-old boy. This child had no parents; his mother had already died of AIDS. He was in foster care, but no one came to rock him, hold him, or spend time with him. It broke my heart each day as I cared for him. I watched as others rocked and held the children around him in the hospital, but no one—*no one*—volunteered to hold him or even touch him. I tried to get those in the room to hold and rock this baby also, but no one would. So I put out a call for some women in our missions organization to help.

Within hours—literally hours—women were waiting to rock and hold this baby. They came in shifts. They rocked him. They sang to him. They played with him.

They were there when he died.

With humility on their faces and love pouring from a Source greater than themselves, they touched him. They connected with and blessed him. They reassured him in his fear, and cleansed his disease-racked body. As he drew his last breaths, they reassured him that he was safe and loved as they passed him from one set of loving arms to the arms of Jesus. And they did so with the steadfast hope that he is ultimately healed, and free at last.

They touched because they loved. But oh, how they love because they touched.

For Reflection and Discussion

1. Have you ever had the opportunity to shake hands or get a hug from somebody famous, or somebody you looked up to greatly? Who was it, and how did that make you feel?

2. In Mark 10:13–16, why do you think the disciples rebuked the parents, and what was the message Jesus was sending by touching the children?

3. Matthew 17:7 describes the reassuring touch of Jesus to Peter when he was frightened. What is an example of how someone has calmed your fears or reassured you at a stressful or frightening time?

4. What are some ways we can bear the physical burdens of people who are sick or disabled? Read Galatians 6:2.

5. What are some barriers or challenges you face when it comes to touching the lives of others? What fears, anxieties, distractions, or false beliefs make it challenging to reach out and touch someone in Jesus's name?

Chapter 6

Thinking with His Mind

The sound of his voice made her blood seem to freeze. He was older now—a balding, heavyset man in a gray overcoat. But Corrie remembered the blue uniform and visored cap with its skull and crossbones. Memories of Ravensbruck returned with a rush: the shame, fear, pain, and death. The Nazis had arrested Corrie ten Boom and her sister Betsie for concealing Jews in their home during the occupation of Holland. Now, two years after the war's end, she had been speaking in a church in Munich and stood looking into the eyes of her former captor, his hand outstretched.

"A fine message, fraulein! How good it is to know that, as you say, all our sins are at the bottom of the sea!" It was Corrie's first encounter with a former guard.

"You mentioned Ravensbruck in your talk," he said. "I was a guard there. But since that time I have become a Christian. I know that God has forgiven me for the cruel things I did there, but I would like to hear it from your lips as well. Fraulein, will you forgive me?" Again the hand reached out.

Memories of Betsie's death in the camp haunted her. How

could this man erase that memory simply for the asking? Corrie knew what Jesus taught about forgiveness, yet she paused for what seemed an eternity, facing the hardest thing she'd ever been asked to do. With coldness still

His offer is extravagantly merciful.

clutching her heart and a prayer to God for help, she made a choice of her will. Woodenly, mechanically, she thrust her hand into his. As she did, something incredible happened. In Corrie's words, "The current started in my shoulder, raced down my arm, sprang into our joined hands. And then this healing warmth seemed to flood my whole being, bringing tears to my eyes. 'I forgive you, brother!' I cried. 'With all my heart!'"

For a long moment they grasped each other's hands, the former captor and former prisoner. Never had she known God's love so intensely as she did then.

Because she had experienced God's love and forgiveness, Corrie thought differently. She learned that loving with God's heart is the result of thinking with God's mind. That's one of the reasons God gave us His Word—to tell us what He's thinking. He makes it clear in both the Old and New Testaments that He thinks differently than the way humans tend to think. To know what He's thinking, you have to be in His Word and in communication with Him. You have to know Him and His thoughts, in order to love like Him.

When Jesus gave the Great Commandment, He spoke about loving God with our minds and loving our neighbor as ourselves (Matthew 22:37–39). Both of these involve the way we filter and process information. He also promises us the capacity to think with His thoughts (1 Corinthians 2:16). When we think with the mind of Christ, we are able to express God's love in a way that's impossible when left to human reasoning. In this chapter we'll explore how God thinks differently, and how entering into that type of thinking will empower you and me to love as Jesus loved.

Through the prophet Isaiah, the Lord passionately offered Israel His mercy and forgiveness.

Seek the LORD while He may be found;
call to Him while He is near.
Let the wicked one abandon his way,
and the sinful one his thoughts;
let him return to the LORD,
so He may have compassion on him,
and to our God, for He will freely forgive.
"For My thoughts are not your thoughts,
and your ways are not My ways."
This is the LORD's declaration.
"For as heaven is higher than earth,
so My ways are higher than your ways,
and My thoughts than your thoughts.
For just as rain and snow fall from heaven,
and do not return there
without saturating the earth,
and making it germinate and sprout,
and providing seed to sow
and food to eat,
so My word that comes from My mouth
will not return to Me empty,
but it will accomplish what I please,
and will prosper in what I send it to do."
—Isaiah 55:6–11

God describes His thoughts as higher than ours, but accessible through intimacy with Him. His thinking is characterized by forgiveness, faithfulness, and fulfilled purpose.

Thinking in Terms of Forgiveness

The Bible is about what God did in order for us to be forgiven. His offer is extravagantly merciful. Several Old Testament passages use different figures of speech to describe the extent of God's forgiveness of our sins. The psalmist points out that He has removed our transgressions from us as far as the east is from the west (Psalm 103:12). Isaiah declares that God kept him from the pit of destruction, and had put all his sins behind God's back (Isaiah 38:17). Micah said that the Lord would tread our sins underfoot and hurl all our iniquities into the depths of the sea (Micah 7:19). And again through Isaiah, the Lord speaks of blotting out our transgressions (removing them from His record) and remembering them no more (Isaiah 43:25).

All Christians stand in a position of being forgiven. God's forgiveness is something that is freely given, not earned. Certainly that should affect the way we see ourselves. But it should also affect the way we see other believers. They are just as forgiven as we are! And because we have been greatly forgiven by God, we can forgive others as well. Paul says in Ephesians 4:32, "Be kind and compassionate to one another, forgiving one another, just as God also forgave you in Christ."

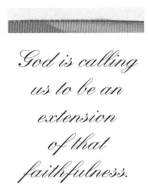

God is calling us to be an extension of that faithfulness.

Because God thinks in terms of forgiveness, we are empowered to extend His forgiveness to those who need it. When God looks at any unsaved person, He sees someone who needs His forgiveness. That's what got Jesus in so much trouble with the establishment of His day. Jesus brought a whole new perspective on lost people. *They saw* a woman caught in adultery, greedy and dishonest tax collectors, or people who brought distractions and disruptions into their houses of worship. *Jesus saw* people in need of forgiveness.

When we see our frustrations, disappointments, or painful experiences as forgiveness opportunities, we're beginning to think as God thinks. Truly, these opportunities to forgive show up most frequently at home.

Forgiveness is essential in a marriage. It enables wives and husbands to grow in their love for each other. Mark is the best at saying "I am sorry"—even when it isn't his fault. He doesn't want any conflict between us, and knows that forgiveness is necessary in love relationships. Mark and I also love our children unconditionally. Our love isn't based on what they do or don't do; we love them. Over the course of their teenage years, we had, as most families do, a few bumps along the way. However, the children knew that our love was not dependent on how they acted. They found safety in our forgiveness as they were able to come to us with any problem, large or small. We are now seeing that same unconditional love that we demonstrated to them in their relationships and marriages, and with their children.

Thinking in Terms of Faithfulness

I attended high school at the International School of Bangkok, but I had to come back to the States for college. I didn't particularly want to do so, but it was necessary. As I prepared to leave for Texas, I read in Habakkuk 1:5 a promise from the Lord about His accomplishing a work in my day that I couldn't believe. It seemed as if He were speaking that promise to me personally, and I held on to it. I came to a strange place, where I didn't know one single person. As I mentioned earlier, I didn't know how to drive, nor did I understand the ways of Americans in the United States. However, by providing new friends and people to help take care of me and to stand in as my parents, God was faithful to provide all I needed in this new home on the other side of the world.

Through Isaiah, God is saying that He is faithful to keep His promises, even though we are tempted to think He won't. Because He does, we can be secure in the face of temptation (1 Corinthians 10:13). We have the power to do anything God has called us to do (1 Thessalonians 5:24). We don't have to measure God's faithfulness by our unfaithfulness (2 Timothy 2:13). And we are important enough to our God that He will keep His promises to us (Hebrews 10:23).

Other believers need God's faithfulness as much as we do, and God is calling us to be an extension of that faithfulness. When other Christians are facing temptation, we should be an extension of God's security. When someone is seeking to serve the Lord, we should be an extension of God's encouragement. When another Christian is unfaithful, we need to show that person that we'll be faithful anyway. When a fellow believer is struggling, we need to show that person that he or she is important to God, and to us.

God's faithfulness, expressed through believers who think like Him, extends hope to a hopeless world. When God looks at unbelievers, He sees people whose lives have been dashed to pieces on the rocks of broken promises. They've been lied to by the world and sometimes ignored by the Christians, and all they have left is hopelessness. They believed the promise of pleasure, materialism, or ego, and were greatly disappointed. They need to know that there is still someone who keeps His promises, who will never fail them or forsake them. But they won't believe that God is faithful until they see that we are.

Missionaries around the world model that. They leave family and comfort, often to serve Christ in very hard places. They go on the promise that God will help them, guide them, and go before them. They remain faithful to Him even when things seem hopeless. They daily claim the Lord's promises as they are His hands and heart to a lost world. Their trust in God's faithfulness and their willingness to think in terms of faithfulness enables them to love in humanly impossible situations.

Thinking in Terms of Fulfilled Purpose

It was an eye-opening day. My sisters and I accompanied my parents on a mobile clinic in the more remote parts of Thailand. We put a Vacation Bible School (VBS) together for the kids while they waited to see the doctor. We used items sent to us by a group of women back in the States who, though they couldn't come to Thailand, were there through the items they sent and the praying they did. They sent us everything we needed for the VBS: craft items, stories with visual helps, M&M's for snacks. We even used the box it all came in. These children were sick and looked malnourished. They were also starving for attention and hungry for what was missing in their lives. The teenagers there, who were about our age, saw no way out of the poverty they were in. They saw no meaning or purpose to their lives.

We had a chance to tell them about the One in whom they did have a purpose, who gives meaning and a reason for living. We talked about their unique gifts. Many were master craftsmen at young ages; many others were already good at farming. One of the missionaries there preached to the group about love, saying that the doctors and nurses were there helping because they loved Jesus and that enabled them to love everyone there that day. Around a palm tree at that medical site, many teenagers opened their hearts to the love God so freely offered them. They left there full of hope and wanting to share that love. They were filled with the love of a God of purpose.

God's ultimate purpose is to bring the world to a saving knowledge of Christ. He's not willing that any should perish

(2 Peter 3:9). While we tend to see people in terms of their labels or masks, God sees people for whom He has a plan. We are programmed by our society to think in terms of chance, luck, and coincidence. God thinks, speaks, and acts with purpose. Paul told the Philippian Christians, "I am sure of this, that He who started a good work in you will carry it on to completion until the day of Christ Jesus" (Philippians 1:6). Aren't you glad God finishes what He starts? And He never squanders a growth opportunity!

Our circumstances or failures haven't surprised Him.

God is, has always been, and will always be a God of purpose. Our circumstances or failures haven't surprised Him. He has felt every emotion we have ever felt, with much more intensity. He hasn't dumped us, quit on us, or forgotten us. He isn't getting mad or getting even. But I will say what He *is* doing. He's teaching us to build our hope in Him and to fall in love with eternal things, not the temporal things of this world. He's teaching us to walk by faith, in the fullness of His power. He's teaching us to be accountable to Him for what we say and how we live. He's using us and our circumstances to show an unbelieving world that Jesus saves. He's teaching us to be servants, and to love even the unlovely. And He's teaching us to live under His authority and lordship.

Thinking in terms of fulfilled purpose not only helps in dealing with circumstances, it also helps us be as patient with others as God is with us, as I've experienced in my family After having three girls, we were excited to prepare a boy's room for a new baby. John Mark came home to his boyish room, painted in boy colors, with an expensive boyish bear border around the room at child eye level so he could enjoy it when he was older. That day eventually came, and he used to love to touch and pat the bears. He named them all. Then one day I came in and saw him holding a permanent marker in his hand. He had drawn all over every one of the bears. He looked at me with such big brown happy eyes and said, "Look, Mama. I gave the bears a happy mark!"

I knew I had a choice. I could make this a good teaching moment. I took this option and we talked about the bears and how not to mark on them. "But, Mama," he said, I 'lubvd' them so much that I wanted to show them I loved them. I helped them color!" To this day, my son remembers the time he loved those bears and didn't get spanked. Love sometimes has to think big picture when a wrong has been done. It meant more to him that I loved the bears, too, and didn't get mad at him. He says that was his debut as an artist!

The Mind of Christ—Unity

Paul encouraged the Philippians to think like Christ. By doing so, they would love like Christ.

> If then there is any encouragement in Christ, if any consolation of love, if any fellowship with the Spirit, if any affection and mercy, fulfill my joy by thinking the same way, having the same love, sharing the same feelings, focusing on one goal. Do nothing out of rivalry or conceit, but in humility consider others as more important than yourselves. Everyone should look out not only for his own interests, but also for the interests of others.
>
> Make your own attitude that of Christ Jesus, who, existing in the form of God, did not consider equality with God as something to be used for His own advantage. Instead He emptied Himself by assuming the form of a slave, taking on the likeness of men. And when He had come as a man in His external form, He humbled Himself by becoming obedient to the point of death—even to death on a cross.
> —Philippians 2:1–8

When we think with the mind of Christ, unity will be our theme. Jesus Himself prayed for Christians of our day, that we would be one, just as He was one with the Father (John 17:21). Unity doesn't mean we always agree. Paul described it as "thinking the same way, having the same love, sharing the same feelings, focusing on one goal." Thinking the same way has more to do with our attitudes toward our ideas than with the ideas themselves.

Having the same love means having the same values; while we may not agree on everything, we are committed in love to each other as persons. Sharing the same feelings involves having the same priorities about things. And focusing on one goal means deciding what our mission is and together setting about doing it.

This was illustrated in the lives of some believers in a Muslim-controlled country that was closed to sharing the gospel. In fact, if believers in Jesus were known or discovered, they were imprisoned or worse. In spite of those risks, however, a North American woman felt the Lord's calling to go into this country. What followed was an amazing display of support and unity, at great risk to believers there. While many Muslims there hated Americans, they wanted their children to learn to speak English. With the help of some in-country believers, one of the private schools sent out a request for an English

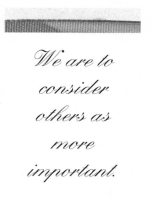

We are to consider others as more important.

teacher. The woman with the calling applied, and finally received a visa to enter the country and soon started her journey there. At great risk to themselves, other believers in the country found her a place to live above a Muslim family. It was a team effort to get things going in this dark place that needed to know Jesus. Why would they risk their lives to help this worker? Because they knew she would have an impact for the Lord at this school where future leaders were being taught. And they knew she couldn't accomplish this on her own.

When my second daughter was about to give birth, her family was all she had for support. Mark and I went to be with her during her labor and delivery. My oldest daughter was a delivery room nurse; and although she was off that day, she came in to be her sister's nurse. Soon her other siblings appeared, after driving several hours. They all came to be there when she gave birth to our grandson. I was proud of the support and family teamwork they showed when Julie needed our support and presence. It was a wonderful day, and God's wonderful blessing of our grandson was born that day. It took a family to get him here!

Whether in the early church, today's last frontier, or a typical American family, unity makes love possible. When we lay down our own agendas and make them subservient to God's call to focus on one heart and purpose, love flows!

The Mind of Christ—Humility

The mind of Christ is characterized by humility. Jesus humbled Himself by becoming obedient to the point of death on a cross. Now, in the same humility, we are to consider others as more important than ourselves. This humility literally means the mentality of a common slave. How does a slave think? Like someone who is completely emptied of his rights, and who considers others as more important than himself. Jesus embraced this way of thinking when He, being God, emptied Himself and took on the form of a slave.

Have you ever considered how many painful relationships arise from people insisting on their "rights"? Have you ever said, or heard someone else say, "I have a right to be angry!"? Maybe you do, but to walk in love, you'll give up that right. Yes, maybe we have a right to our own opinion, to say what we think, or to spend our money however we wish. But thinking with the mind of Christ means deliberately laying down what we perceive to be our rights and thinking differently about ourselves. It means changing our expectations about how others should treat us or respond to us.

My husband is a great example of humility. He is always putting others first. He wants no recognition for himself. Even as a famous Arkansas football player and a great golfer today, he always downplays what he can do and how well he does it. He's a great example for our children to see what it means to put others first. I have seen this as well on the missions field in many areas. Most of the missionaries I have met are always putting the needs of others above themselves as well as about their own families for the sake of the gospel.

The Mind of Christ—Servanthood

Thinking with the mind of Christ means choosing to lay down that personal sense of entitlement and actually give it to someone else. That is the nature of servanthood—actually thinking in terms of serving the needs and interests of others. The mind of Christ carries with it a quality of love that directs more energy toward others' concerns than toward our own well-being. Nominal Christians and unbelievers are capable of great acts of kindness, but only the believer with the mind of Christ can be concerned with another's longings more than with his or her own.

Servants have a bias toward action, and meeting the needs of others first. One of the best examples of this was a physician named Martha Myers. Dr. Martha, as she was known, served as a missionary in Yemen. She frequently drove her land cruiser through the mountains of Yemen, immunizing children and dispensing medicine to the poor. She was greeted with shouts of "Dr. Martha" wherever she traveled. Though aware of the danger of publicly serving Christ in a Muslim nation, Martha's love for the people kept her serving there.

People were drawn to her because they sensed that she truly cared about them. She understood people and their problems, and her love showed in her face and in her actions.

Martha's servanthood reached beyond her medical skills. On one occasion, she gave her savings account to help pay the cost of a kidney transplant for one of the hospital patients. She loved the Yemeni people so much; she had even requested to be buried there. Her wish was granted.

On December 30, 2002, Martha was one of three missionaries killed when a gunman smuggled a rifle into the hospital where she worked. She gave her life for the people she loved and those she wanted to know Jesus. It would have been easy for her to leave, but she knew that by being a servant among her people group, she would model the love of Jesus. Martha was buried on the hospital grounds as a reminder to all the people of Yemen that she and Jesus loved them. She always put her patients and the people of Yemen first.

In a January 16, 2003, article published in the *Florida Baptist Witness,* Jennifer Davis Rash, managing editor of the *Alabama Baptist* wrote, "During the funeral 40,000 Yemeni nationals gathered at the hospital and lined the street for a half-mile outside the hospital gates to pay their respects." Rash wrote that Martha's life exemplified Jesus Christ, "and in a country where professing faith in Jesus Christ could result in death, mourners sang 'He Is

Lord' in Arabic and recited the Lord's Prayer." Because a woman loved as Jesus loved, touched as Jesus touched, thought as Jesus thought, Yemenis have a chance to know of His love. She thought it was worth it! Because she thought as He thought.

The Lord has convicted me to pray for my neighbors even more intentionally lately. I don't know them all very well, but I am working on knowing them better. In the meantime, I pray for them and their families, and am praying for opportunities to be His example in our neighborhood. Since I've been doing that, I have had more opportunities to visit with them. My Muslim friend has been more open to conversations about Jesus. She recently asked about my grandson, wanting to know why on earth we would want him and his mother to live with us. I told her that it was Jesus's love in us that enables us to love them. I told her what an expression of God's love it was for Julie that He gave her a son to raise despite hard circumstances. That Julie was our daughter, and nothing that happened to our children or grandson would make us love them any less.

She talked about how love was conditional in her country. There was no assurance of love from day to day. It could be there one day and gone the next. Even worse, someone could be loved one day and killed the next. She couldn't understand the kind of love that we have for our families and children—or the kind that Jesus has for us. She said she was too bad and ugly for anyone to love her. It was the perfect opening for me to tell her about the love that Jesus offers.

In our own love, we can't possibly love as Jesus loves. Only as we learn to see from His perspective—forgiveness, faithfulness, and fulfilled purpose—and to think with the mind of Christ—unity, humility, servanthood—can we be empowered to love that boldly and freely.

I'll keep praying—and trust God to keep opening doors to love—wherever I walk.

For Reflection and Discussion

1. Compare the way you tend to think with the way someone from another generation, region, or culture thinks. How are you alike? How are you different?

2. Read Matthew 18:21–35. What makes forgiveness more difficult to offer than it is to ask for?

3. Why do you think unity among the people of God is so important to Jesus? Read John 17:20–21.

4. Why do you think Jesus refers to servants as the greatest in the kingdom? Read Matthew 23:11–12. What makes a servant different and valuable?

5. This chapter mentions six unique ways that we think with the mind of Christ: forgiveness, faithfulness, fulfilled purpose, unity, humility, and servanthood. Which of these presents the biggest challenge to you at this time, and why?

Chapter 7

Feeling with His Heart

Three big travel buses slowed to a stop, the doors opened, and out popped a tired little boy.

"Is this where I live now?"

The words came out of his mouth with hardly a thought. Behind him was a very tired young woman, carrying a little baby and pulling behind her the only possessions she had left. As people got off the bus, they wandered around the camp in a state of shock. This was the third stop in a long journey since Hurricane Katrina had ravaged Louisiana. After cabin assignments were made, health forms filled out, and a snack eaten, this young mom and her children headed for their new "home."

As I watched her walk so slowly toward her cabin, tears running down her face, a group of women moved toward her. Someone offered to carry the baby. Another woman put out her hand to lead the little boy. Still another offered a tissue to dry the tears, while yet another put her arms around this young mom and walked with and hugged her as they went. The face and heart of Jesus was throughout the camp as volunteers ministered to those whose hearts were breaking and whose lives had been turned upside down. A touch here, a cup of cold water there—people who loved the Lord were reaching out in His name to say they cared. In the lives of so many who didn't know where to begin, caring Christians allowed themselves to *feel* the concern of Christ for people in pain.

This scene was being repeated not only in my home state of Arkansas, but throughout the states affected by the storm and in those that received evacuees. Agencies, churches, groups, and individuals delivered myriad services. Some went to the front lines of the destruction to distribute food, blankets, medical supplies, and care. Some offered to relocate evacuees, either temporarily or permanently. Many gave money or other tangible resources. Others prayed faithfully. Yet, regardless of the activity, all the helpers had one thing in common: they allowed their hearts to feel someone else's pain and the Lord's passion.

It's difficult to heal what we can't feel.

The New Testament makes it clear that love is a verb—it is something you *do*. I fear that we sometimes overlook that component of love that stimulates us to loving actions by causing us to *feel*. Empathy and sympathy, passion and compassion are love-driving emotional forces, if we allow them to be. We serve a Savior who was *moved* by the concerns, sufferings, and dreams of others. Can we, who claim to follow Him, be no less? Are we moved to show compassion?

Years ago, Steve Camp cowrote and sang a haunting song about AIDS victims. The song still rings true today, not only in its story about victims of a terrible disease, but also about feeling the pain of a hurting world.

It's difficult to heal what we can't feel. It's nearly impossible to love by "talking about the love of God but judging those who need it most" as Camp wrote. We serve a great High Priest who was "touched with the feeling of our infirmities" (Hebrews 4:15 KJV). He wants us to be touched as well, and that's what this chapter is all about.

A New Look at a Popular Word

Passion is in. It's a popular word in religious circles, on the motivational speaking circuit, and in athletic departments on school campuses. It's in movie and book titles. It's used to describe the singles dating scene; a student-led worship movement; and a happy, fulfilled life. As it is with most popular words, *passion* gets tossed around in so many ways that it's easy to lose its most important meanings. Phrases such as "passionately in love," "passionate about football," or "you are so passionate about . . ." are used every day.

I married one of those "passionate about football" types, but he came by it honestly. Mark was a football player at the University of Arkansas. I have learned a bit about passion for Razorback football from him. Win or lose, he leaves no doubt where he stands. And during key moments in games, it's actually safer to move all the furniture away so he and my family can jump around!

With all the different uses and ideas of what *passion* is about, I decided to look it up in the dictionary and was quite surprised at what I found. According to *Webster's Third New International Dictionary*, Unabridged, *passion* can mean: "the sufferings of a martyr; the sufferings of Jesus between the night of the Last Supper and his death including the agony in Gethsemane; violent, intense, or overmastering emotion; a state of or capacity for emotional excitement."

Does that definition surprise you? Does that change your mind on being passionately in love, considering that would mean you would be "suffering" or in "agony"? It is this kind of passionate love that God has for us. First John 4:10 says that "love consists in this: not that we loved God, but that He loved us and sent His Son to be the propitiation for our sins." This was a love strong enough to suffer through the loss of His only Son, love enough to be a martyr for our sins, love enough to go through the agony of the Cross, love enough to celebrate the excitement of the Resurrection. This love is fueled by its suffering, concern, and "intense emotional drive." I saw it in the urgency my parents had about sharing Jesus that they passed on to me. I've seen it in other missionaries too. Ginger Smith, a missionary in inner-city Houston, has such an urgency about her to share Christ with those who are lost. Every day that intense urgency drives her to minister to the physical and spiritual needs of those around her. She loves as Jesus loves.

You and I can't offer what we don't have. So from where does passion come? How can we be touched as Jesus was touched? The following PASSION acrostic has been helpful to me in gaining and sustaining passion in the truest sense of the word.

P—Praying

Do you talk on the phone at least once a day? We all do. With cell phones, we are accessible 24 hours a day. You can't eat out, shop, drive, or go to a ball game without seeing people on their cell phones. Imagine if we were to spend as much time talking to God in prayer as to people on cell phones! Isn't it amazing that we have unlimited accessibility to God? No roaming fees, no overage, and no dropped calls!

Seriously, prayer is our connection to God. It is our chance to share our hearts with Him and, just as important, His opportunity to share His heart with us. Prayer is often the means by which we discern His will. The Book of Esther tells the story of a queen who relied on God through prayer. Mordecai, Esther's cousin, learned of a conspiracy to kill all the Jews, which would include Mordecai and Esther. Mordecai went to Esther, pleading for intervention as the wife of the king. For Esther to go to the king without him requesting her could have meant death. Can you imagine a marriage in which the husband had the power to have his wife killed any time she went in to talk with him if he didn't first ask for her?

At first Esther did not want to take the kind of risk Mordecai was asking of her. But Mordecai challenged her with this statement: "Don't think that you will escape the fate of all the Jews because you are in the king's palace. If you keep silent at this time, liberation and deliverance will come to the Jewish people from another place, but you and your father's house will be destroyed. Who knows, perhaps you have come to the kingdom for such a time as this" (Esther 4:13–14).

You may not feel as though your life is as historically dramatic, but we all can trace experiences and events that have prepared us for God's ultimate plan for our lives. Not a single minute of our lives is wasted when we allow God to use them for His purposes.

Before Esther went into the inner court to see the king, she took time to pray. Not just a few minutes beforehand—she actually spent three *days* in prayer and fasting. No doubt she was pleading to God for His mercies, but also checking her own heart and motives for what she was about to do. Was she being selfish and saving her own life or were the Jews as a whole her primary motive? Moreover, not only did Esther pray herself, but she also requested the prayers of others. "Where two are three are gathered" (Matthew 18:20) was true then as it is now. As Esther and her intercessors prayed and fasted, she felt even more deeply God's heart for His people. At the end of her time in prayer, she was ready to present herself to the king, trusting the outcome to God. "If I perish, I perish!" she declared (Esther 4:16).

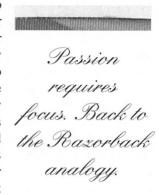

Passion requires focus. Back to the Razorback analogy.

After her time in prayer, Esther knew God was with her. Sometimes in our own lives we find ourselves doubting and wondering. Perhaps it is because we have not yet taken the time to know God's presence in prayer. When we "pray constantly" (1 Thessalonians 5:17)—when our connection with Him is open 24/7—it is amazing how our confidence changes. At that point, it's not about us and what we're doing, but about God and what *He* is doing.

A—Actively in His Word

How can a young man keep his way pure?
By keeping Your word.
I have sought You with all my heart;
don't let me wander from Your commands.
—Psalm 119:9–10

Passion requires focus. Back to the Razorback analogy. You will never find my husband cheering for the Texas Longhorns—ever! He is very much focused on his alma mater, and that drives his passion.

To be passionate about Christ, we have to be focused on Christ. That can only happen when we are in His Word. Mason, our grandson, is absolutely smitten with the Disney character Nemo. He loves that animated fish! When Nemo is on, his eyes are fixed. It doesn't matter what you put in front of him, he is honed in on Nemo, and nothing else is tempting.

That's what God's Word does for us. It keeps us focused. No matter what else is dangled in front of us, we are not tempted. It's interesting that David wrote the preceding words in Psalm 119. This was the same David who fell in a big way when he was unfocused on God and focused instead on Bathsheba. David knew that focus on God's Word keeps our hearts focused. I heard someone say recently our hearts long to be full of passion, so if God is not filling that space, our hearts will wander in search of it. When God's Word fills every inch of our hearts, there is no need to wander. We are focused. How can we keep our way pure in a world that honors impurity? By living according to His Word. This requires intentional time in reading, studying, meditating on, and being refreshed by the truth of Scripture. Not reading it like a catalog or encyclopedia, but like a love letter written specifically to you.

S—Submission

You've gotta love that word! Most women immediately think of being submissive to their husbands, and couples may think of being submitted to one another, but there's a higher call to submission than that. Being submissive to the Lord means being able to give it all up, including our own desires and feelings, to pursue His call and purpose. That is what *passion* is all about—sacrificing our desires for His.

If you're a parent, have you ever given up something so that your child could have something? Have you given up sleep to stay up with a sick child? How many wives have given up watching a movie and watched the game instead? Or how many husbands have trudged along in the mall with wife and a smile, honestly wanting be somewhere else? Most of us can answer yes to at least one of those questions. That is being submissive—giving something up for someone else's benefit. If you answered yes to one of those questions, did you regret your decision? Doubtful. It is at that point that another's joy is more valuable than our own.

Mary, the mother of Jesus, is a wonderful example of being submissive to God's will. Imagine what it must have been like for her to be told she was pregnant at the ripe old age of 14 or 15, with no husband—only the promise of one. And once she was pregnant, Joseph could have withdrawn his promise and no one would have faulted his decision. Mary had choices. She could have lied about the situation. She could have refused. She could have done any number of things, but she chose to submit to God's plan for her life and carry this child. Her submission paid off. Not only did she have the honor of carrying and raising Jesus, she knew the Savior of the world from day one!

Submission is not always about doing; sometimes it involves a change in attitude. Sometimes it is about being kind when everything in us wants to be vengeful. It's about giving up personal time to spend time with God. It's about budgeting our resources in a manner that matters for eternity, not just today's satisfaction. Submission—releasing your own will to God's in order for His glory to be seen and known by others—is an important key to developing passion for the things that matter most.

Passion follows service. To increase your passion . . . try acts of service.

S—Servant's Heart

Passion follows service. If you want to increase your passion for anything or anyone, try acts of service or kindness for them. Jesus Himself was the greatest servant ever known, and He taught the disciples that the greatest in the kingdom were the servants (Matthew 20:26). Mary and Martha of Bethany are also great examples of servanthood. Though they attended to the Lord Jesus in different ways, their uniquely expressed service only increased their passion for Him and His kingdom.

My greatest personal example of someone who embodied a servant's heart is my dad. I speak of him often because he was my first demonstration of the concept of servanthood. As a gifted surgeon and physician, my dad could have had a practice anywhere in United States, but he chose to be obedient to God and to go away from his homeland to do so. Practicing in Thailand, he

Being a servant takes practice.

looked for ways to serve the Thai people every day. Most often that was with medical care, but not always. Sometimes it was providing a family with food, or praying over a sick child. Sometimes it was serving someone clean drinking water, or taking a leper's diseased and drawn hand in his and praying to the God of healing to help this friend of his. My dad's life was spent not serving himself but serving others.

Operating rooms in Thailand were not air-conditioned in the early days. Most days, the temperatures are over 100°F, with relative humidity nearing 100 percent. Not once did I hear my dad complain about that. I only heard him wish for more time to be able to help more people. Every day he began on his knees, asking the Lord how he could serve the Lord and the Thai people. Oh, how passionate he was about wanting each person to hear the name Jesus! That passion taught me the urgency of sharing the name Jesus with people everywhere.

Although no longer in Thailand, my parents continue to be missionaries in west Texas to those that need to hear the name Jesus. Through church planting and service, they both continue to serve anyone and everyone at their point of need. That even involved my dad coming out of retirement to serve as the medical director of the Community Health Center of Lubbock, offering medical care to all who seek it, regardless of their ability to pay. This model of service influenced me and my siblings as well.

On December 26, 2004, a destructive tsunami consumed much of southern Thailand, as well as Indonesia, Sri Lanka, and India. It was one of the most devastating natural disasters in history, ultimately killing more than 225,000 people. Watching the news, my sister Robin knew that for the first time in 34 years, it was time to return to the land of her childhood. And who better to take on a medical service team than some of the people who taught her servanthood as a child? Together with my dad and my other sister, a team of 14 volunteers from Texas and Alabama returned to serve the medical, psychological, economic, and spiritual needs of the survivors. Because Daddy was still licensed to practice medicine in Thailand, he could take the team to places that most other relief workers could not go. As a result of that effort, passion for Thailand and the Thai people has deepened greatly. Businesses have been restored, homes rebuilt, a children's center built, and a church planted, with many people coming to Christ.

Being a servant takes practice. We have to learn to see needs and we have to learn to be disciplined enough to do something about those needs. It isn't necessary to wait until a cataclysmic disaster strikes before we practice servanthood. We can look for ways to express love through acts of kindness. As we do, the passion—and love—will follow.

I—Involved in the Lives of Others

No, I don't mean being a busybody! I am talking about pouring our lives into others. I already mentioned in chapter 3 how Jesus gained His perspective through involvement. Parents do this every day in the lives of children and spouses. Awareness—and involvement—in the big and small details of our loved ones lives increases our sensitivity to their needs.

Another biblical example of involvement is Rahab. We encounter this remarkable woman in the Book of Joshua (Joshua 2:1–21). Rahab was a prostitute who lived in Jericho. She had the foresight to recognize that the true God was with the Israelites and that Jericho's days were numbered. She involved her life with two Israelite spies whom she didn't even know by taking them in and hiding them. The king of Jericho heard about these men and went to Rahab. No two ways about it, she lied to the king and sent him on a wild-goose chase. She sensed something different about these men who had come to her. She responded to them, "I know that the LORD has given you this land and that dread of you has fallen on us . . . for the LORD your God is God in heaven above and on earth below" (Joshua 2:9, 11). She went on to ask them to be kind to her when the land were taken. The men responded with an interesting answer: "We will give our lives for yours. If you don't report our mission, we will show kindness and faithfulness to you when the LORD gives us the land" (Joshua 2:14).

In a time when others in the city were closing themselves off, boarding up their homes, and fortifying their city, Rahab became *involved* in the lives of the spies. And God blessed her involvement. Sometimes when we invest in the lives of others, it all works out great. Other times it brings heartache. But we can never be passionate from a distance. We have to be involved, regardless of the outcome. Remember the definition—"emotional excitement"? That is what compels us to be involved with others. Caring, sharing, laughing, crying, playing, working—involved together!

O—On Mission

A person with passion will always be on mission. And a person on mission will never wonder what happened to his or her passion! Every thought, word, and action will be about completing that one thing about which they are so passionate. For God, it is about bringing people to Himself. From Genesis to Revelation, the Bible is filled with the record of God bringing people to Himself. All the miracles were to show His great power. All the changed lives were demonstrating His love. This all culminated in the ultimate mission—the life, death, resurrection, and ascension of Jesus Christ.

Being on mission is having purpose. For some, that means a call to be a *missionary*. For most of us, it's being on mission in our everyday lives—showing the fruit of the Spirit in our lives at work. Showing what it is to have a quiet time to our kids by modeling that for them. Saying a word of encouragement at the grocery store or doctor's office. Using our vacation time to go on disaster relief, teach Vacation Bible School, or to hang out with a group of kids or teenagers at camp.

We find a picture of a woman on mission in Proverbs 31. She took care of her children, husband, family, community, and business—all for the purpose of bringing glory to God. She established trust in her marriage, practiced daily diligence and sought value in her personal and business finances, avoided procrastination by taking early action—even before sunrise. She made decisions based on what she wanted from the future, not just as a consumer for the moment; invested time in maintaining her health and strength; and was generous with the poor and needy.

She was wise enough to establish multiple streams of income, and she won her children's affection and admiration.

What drove this woman? What was the mission that compelled her? In language easily overlooked, verse 30 indicates that she reverenced God. Her mission came from her Maker!

No matter where we live physically, we are all called to be on mission; it is a command for the believer. Our missions may vary, but the Sender remains the same. And faithfulness to the mission will only serve to increase our passion.

We don't have the luxury of waiting.

N—Now

Some of us are known for wanting to have all our ducks in a row before moving on to the next project. Unfortunately, in living and passing on spiritual passion, we don't have the luxury of waiting for that to happen. We live in a world in which two-thirds of the population—more than 4.5 *billion* lost people (according to Todd Johnson in "World Christian Trends, Update 2007")—need us to be passionate *today*. They don't have time for us to have it all figured out! On top of that, there will be thousands more by tomorrow who need us to be passing on our passion, so that the message of Christ can be told not only today, but in the years to come. *The Passion of the Christ* is not simply a movie; it's a mandate. It is the agony and suffering of our Savior, who with compelling deep emotion was driven to the very end so that we might have the excitement and hope of the Resurrection. He was driven by the urgency of the age and the moment. He said, "We must do the works of Him who sent Me while it is day. Night is coming when no one can work" (John 9:4–5). In the three short years of His public ministry, did Jesus heal every sick person in Israel? No. But He healed many. Did He answer every question about the Bible? No. But He taught the ones who would listen, and equipped His followers to continue the message. Simply put, Jesus took action, based on the "shortness of the day."

Now we, His followers, have this mandate:

Therefore, God's chosen ones, holy and loved, put on heartfelt compassion, kindness, humility, gentleness, and patience, accepting one another and forgiving one another if anyone has a complaint against another. Just as the Lord has forgiven you, so also you must forgive. Above all, put on love—the perfect bond of unity.
—Colossians 3:12–15

Compassion and passion require action. Sometimes, like the proverbial man who is building a raft while he floats down the river, we must act first and figure out the results and details later. We can always be ready to feel what others may be feeling. That's what makes it easy, with the power of the Holy Spirit, to clothe ourselves in love.

In all likelihood, there will be yet another hurricane or tsunami. As in times past, people with tender hearts will respond quickly and generously. Yet that doesn't happen unless we cultivate compassion in the daily issues of our lives. Live with passion *without* the major crisis today. Pray. Be actively engaged with God's Word and submitted to God's agenda. Serve others at every opportunity. Be involved in others' lives, and on mission. And whatever else we do, we can take some kind of action *now*. Then when the big crises occur, loving won't be much of a leap.

For Reflection and Discussion

1. What sort of things do you or the people in your family or household get most passionate about—to the point that they're really excited when things go well, or frustrated when they don't?

2. How does Acts 1:14 describe the attitudes and actions of Christ followers right before Pentecost?

3. What risks did Mary take in being willing to submit to God's plan to be the mother of the Messiah? Read Luke 1:38. How do you think it strengthened her passion for Him?

4. Why and how does Paul say we are to be alert and ready for action in 1 Thessalonians 5:4–11?

5. How would you evaluate your ability to enter into the feelings of others—to be passionate or compassionate with them? Based on the PASSION acrostic, where do you see yourself as strong, and what do you need to ask God to help you to work on?

Part 3

Live It Out

"*Immediately they left the boat and their father and followed Him*"
(*Matthew 4:22*).

Jesus expressed His love for people by seeing potential, qualities, gifts, and opportunities that they didn't see in themselves. He then called it out of them by encouraging them, challenging them to maturity, modeling a lifestyle for them, and stimulating them to action.

Chapter 8

Love Calls

Y ou can do this." I've heard that for years, even when I was tempted not to believe it.

Our parents would tell us we could do anything we set our minds on and trusted the Lord to empower us to do.

Playing piano? "You can do it."

Riding a bicycle? "You can do it."

Practicing tying off surgical knots and stitches on the legs of the dining room table (no kidding!)? "You can do this."

The message continued at Baylor. When Aunt Ann let me know I wasn't alone, and helped me believe in myself and trust the Lord, her message was clear: "You can do this." She helped me believe, even when I wasn't motivated, that I could get my degree, adjust to a new culture, meet new friends, and prepare for my own mission.

When I had little to no concept of myself as a teacher, some women in my church saw something else in me. "You can do this," they said, as they challenged me to be involved in teaching a missions lifestyle to children and teenage girls.

I never had any ambition to be up in front of people speaking, but people in key leadership positions had a different idea. Again and again—first on a state level, then on a national level—the message was the same: "We see something in you that you may or may not see in yourself. Regardless, you can do this!" They showed me ways to improve. They prodded, challenged, and encouraged.

What did all these influential people in my life have in common? They *loved* me with a love that called me out. This was the same kind of love that saw something in those Galilean fishermen and called them out of their old identity into a completely new one:

> As He was walking along the Sea of Galilee, He saw two brothers, Simon, who was called Peter, and his brother Andrew. They were casting a net into the sea, since they were fishermen. "Follow Me," He told them, "and I will make you fish for people!" Immediately they left their nets and followed Him. Going on from there, He saw two other brothers, James the son of Zebedee, and his brother John. They were in a boat with Zebedee their father, mending their nets, and He called them. Immediately they left the boat and their father and followed Him.
> —Matthew 4:18–22

Jesus expressed His love for people by seeing potential, qualities, gifts, and opportunities that they didn't see in themselves. He then called it out of them by encouraging them, challenging them to maturity, modeling a lifestyle for them, and stimulating them to action. Some, such as the fishermen mentioned here, were motivated for such a change. Others, like the rich young ruler, resisted. Many, like the woman caught in adultery, and Zacchaeus, the man caught in deceitful behavior, were completely surprised by Jesus's call. Everyone experienced His calling love in ways unique to them and their situation.

The Lord Jesus now commissions us to love others in the same way, and that's what we'll explore in this chapter. This type of expression does not mean trying to reshape somebody else into *our* preferred image—that's manipulation and controlling behavior. Rather, it is seeing in others what Jesus sees, encouraging others in the directions and gifts that are unique to them, and challenging them in God's highest purposes for their lives.

Paul and Timothy: The Caller and the Called

One of the most remarkable relationships in the Bible took place between Paul and a young disciple he met in the town of Lystra. Timothy, like Paul, was the product of two cultures—Jewish and Greek. He was spoken of highly and had a rich heritage of faith. Though Timothy had a completely different personality and gifts, Paul saw in him qualities that called out love in Paul, and growth in his protégé. Timothy became part of Paul's traveling missionary team, then a trusted stand-in for Paul when he couldn't be in certain places. The Apostle Paul made it clear on more than one occasion that, while he completely trusted Timothy's leadership and ministry skills, he was happier when his son in the faith was actually *with* him. Timothy was with Paul when he wrote many of his epistles, including Romans, Philippians, Colossians, and 1 Thessalonians. Moreover, two of Paul's pastoral epistles, including his last letter before his death, were written *to* Timothy. Even as he neared his entry to heaven, Paul expressed love for his son in the faith by calling him out. By the words he chose, the growth he helped produce, the life he modeled, and the passion he stirred, Paul deeply loved and profoundly shaped his disciple.

From one day to the next, I wondered whether he would live.

Message: A Calling of Words

High school at the International School of Bangkok was often a challenge. Most of my classmates were so-called army brats. Their fathers served in Vietnam and the families lived in Bangkok, so they could be close to the husband/father during R&R times. One particular friend lived a very interesting life, or so he thought. He drank often and lived on the edge. From one day to the next, I wondered whether he would live. We had in common being assigned to an orphanage for one of our class assignments and, for a semester, did a study to write a paper about this orphanage. We went to the orphanage daily to work on this together and talked quite a bit. I had a chance to explain to him why I didn't drink alcohol—why I didn't do what he thought was fun! I had a chance to be a witness by my actions as I rocked and loved the children who craved attention. As the semester progressed, I saw a change in him as he held small children who smiled at him for no apparent reason. That melted his hard-shell exterior that hid his hurt.

He was so afraid that his father was going to be killed at war that he tried to act as though it didn't matter and he didn't care; he acted mean and cool so no one would know how afraid he was. The end of the semester came, and we had to put the paper together. During that time, he asked me why I could be so confident and happy with all the disease and abandoned children around me, the war going on, and people dying every day. That gave me a chance to tell him that because of Jesus, I had confidence; I had the ability to love those who needed a touch from Him and I wasn't afraid of what the future held.

This big, tough young man got down on his face on the dirty floor of the orphanage and asked Jesus to be his Lord. From that instant, he began to live a transformed life; Christ called him out of his old self and gave him a new identity and godly character. To this day, this man continues to live a changed life by modeling and mentoring young men in the armed forces with the love of Jesus Christ. Love called him to a new life, a new way of loving, and a new way of living out God's call on his life.

One of the first resources any of us have at our disposal is our speech. According to *Thayer's Greek-English Lexicon,* the very word for exhort or encourage has as its root the word *call.* Strengthening others begins with what you say. Yet, often we struggle most with, "What do I say to encourage?" Take a look at some of the verbal support Paul gave Timothy (2 Timothy 1:1–13):

- "I love you" (v. 2). Timothy was his beloved son.
- "I thank God for you" (v. 3).
- "I'm praying for you night and day" (v. 3).
- "I can't wait to see you" (v. 4).
- "You're for real" (v. 5).
- "You are a gifted man" (v. 6).
- "You don't have to be afraid" (v. 7).

- "You have God's resources available to you" (v. 7).
- "You don't have to be ashamed" (v. 8).
- "You're part of God's plan" (v. 9).
- "I'll lead the way for you" (vv. 8–12).
- "Hang in there!" (v. 13).

Apparently, these words came at a strategic time in Timothy's life. It appears he had become withdrawn, and perhaps fearful. Using what could have been his last opportunity, Paul summoned the courage, faith, and spiritual power he had once seen in Timothy. In a similar way, you and I have the opportunity to summon confidence, faith, courage, patience, and a host of other qualities in the people we care about, simply by using the gift of encouraging words.

Maturity: A Calling of Multiplication

For 14 years, I taught young girls in the missions education program of our church. Every Wednesday night, we would gather and talk about loving Jesus enough every day to tell others about Him in our daily walk. I then had that same group of girls as teenagers. We continued to teach them how to be on mission with Him every day. We did mission action projects to engage them in missions firsthand. We went on missions trips overseas, to other states here in the United States, and also right at home. The goal was to help them learn a missions lifestyle, not just by telling them about it, but by walking alongside them.

Today, one of those young women has finished college and taken on the role of teaching missions to young teenage girls in our church. She teaches the things she herself learned from me and continues to learn from others. She shows teens how to love those around them. I have seen her grow from a little girl, eager to learn about missions, into a beautiful young woman who loves the Lord with all her heart and is teaching others to do that as well! She was always shy and timid while she was young and as a teenager. She has bloomed into the young woman the Lord designed her to be. She never saw herself as a mentor, but that's exactly what she has become—sharing her life and gifts with new generations of young girls—in a wonderful way.

I have another close friend who, when I first met her, was truly shy. Even with a wonderful family, teaching gifts, attractiveness, and more, she didn't think she could do much with missions as she had never been outside of Arkansas. All she needed was a little encouragement. She has matured into a wonderful speaker and entertainer! She even has developed a comedic character she plays, regularly provoking audiences of thousands of women to laugh—and learn that laughter is great medicine. She travels the world to tell others about Jesus, never missing an opportunity to share His love with those in her path.

These contemporary examples illustrate a principle Paul gave to Timothy: "And what you have heard from me in the presence of many witnesses, commit to faithful men who will be able to teach others also" (2 Timothy 2:2). Paul knew the time was coming when Timothy would need the maturity to flourish without him. This is a lesson every believer must learn. The day will come when the people we tend to lean on will no longer be a part of our lives. Moreover, we have the responsibility to pass our influence for Christ to new generations who will do the same.

Rather than trying to squeeze the people we love into our own personal mold, we are to call them to *their unique expression* of godly maturity. A mature Timothy, no doubt, looked *completely* different from a mature Paul or Peter. What is rewarding for me is seeing how the young women I have taught about living a missions lifestyle have grown to embrace the Lord in unique ways. I have seen them when they hurt, as they struggled, and as they discovered and used the gifts that are uniquely theirs. When the lightbulb goes on in their minds and hearts that the Lord loves them and wants them to live for Him and share that love with others, it's amazing to see their transformation and boldness. These young women are finding their own new and exciting missions journey. They are all different, but they all love Him and want others to know that love.

Modeling: A Calling of Example

I love animals. Where I grew up, we had the usual dogs and cats. We also had a pony, a monkey, some ducks, a pet water buffalo, and a pet turkey. So when I heard this story about animals, it caught my attention. A TV show ran a segment about animals in a South African wildlife preserve. The park rangers were concerned about the slaughter of 39 rare white rhinos. It turned out that the rhinos were killed, not by poachers, but by juvenile delinquents—teenage elephants.

The story began a decade ago when the park could no longer sustain the increasing elephant population. They decided to kill off many of the adult elephants whose young were old enough to survive without them. So the elephants grew up fatherless. As time went on, many of these young elephants roamed together in gangs and began doing things that elephants don't normally do. They threw sticks and water at the rhinos and acted like bullies. Without dominant males, the young bulls exhibited aggressive behavior. A few young males grew especially violent, knocking down rhinos and stepping on them or kneeling on them, crushing the life out of them. Mufato, the gang leader, eventually had to be killed.

Don't we, too, need someone to follow and someone to lead?

The rangers theorized that these teenage elephants were acting badly because they lacked role models. They had no one to teach and guide them. They literally had no footprints to follow. The solution was to bring in a large male to lead them and to counteract their bullying behaviors. Soon the new male established dominance and put the young elephants in their places. The killings stopped. The young males were mentored and saved.

Don't we, too, need someone to follow and someone to lead? Paul offered his own example to Timothy of what he sought to model. "But you have followed my *teaching*, *conduct*, *purpose*, *faith*, *patience*, *love*, and *endurance*," he said (2 Timothy 3:10; emphasis mine).

Children, too, learn by mimicking others. I was on a Family on Mission trip a few years ago when I saw firsthand this modeling and learning. What a joy it was to watch as a grandfather modeled how to show the love of Jesus to those who needed Him as they worked on a broken down house to repair and paint it. He made the truth practical. How wonderful it was to watch a single mother work alongside her son as they cleaned out a food pantry kitchen to prepare to feed the homeless. A father, mother, and several children all took part in a backyard Vacation Bible School. I watched as children mimicked parents; great teaching was happening. I saw a grandmother and granddaughter prayerwalking together. These children were learning how to make a difference in their world because someone was modeling it in front of them.

It's interesting—before Jesus ever said, "*Go ye*," He said, "*Follow Me*." He showed His disciples how to pray, communicate truth, serve, and minister in His name. He became the ultimate model of the life He was calling them to live. His invitation to them was, first, an offer of fellowship and demonstration. His love by example created indelible images in their minds that went far beyond words. Left to themselves, no words could have ever compared to the love-driven portrait Jesus painted for them with His life. It's the same for you and me.

The people in our realms of influence are going to look somewhere for answers. Each of us can be that person who is ready to teach. Others will look for someone to imitate. We can be the example they need. They need *reasons*, not just rules to follow. We can be their model of a purposeful life. They need someone to look to when their confidence is shaken. We can be the encourager of their faith. They need someone to steady them when they're frustrated with people or circumstances. We can show them what patience looks like. They need to *see* love in action. We can be the love they're looking to find. They need a reason not to quit when everything in them says to give up. We can be their example of perseverance. Sometimes the most loving thing we can do is go before them and leave footsteps for them to follow.

Motivation: A Calling to Action

Businesses spend billions of dollars annually to convince us to buy products they promise will change and to make our lives more exciting. If we "use as directed," they tell us, we can become thinner or have a different shape, have more intense eyes, fuller lips, or enviable hair. They tell us we can sharpen our memory skills, become the most organized on our block, get cheap flights and hotels as we travel the world and—with the right vehicle—we'll be able to go places we've never been. At some point, however, someone has to ask for the order. This is where the customer must sign the check, make the call, or place his or her money on the counter. Paul does similarly with Timothy:

Before God and Christ Jesus, who is going to judge the living and the dead, and by His appearing and His kingdom, I solemnly charge you: proclaim the message; persist in it whether convenient or not; rebuke, correct, and encourage with great patience and teaching. For the time will come when they will not tolerate sound doctrine, but according to their own desires, will accumulate teachers for themselves because they have an itch to hear something new. They will turn away from hearing the truth and will turn aside to myths. But as for you, keep a clear head about everything, endure hardship, do the work of an evangelist, fulfill your ministry.

For I am already being poured out as a drink offering, and the time for my departure is close. I have fought the good fight, I have finished the race, I have kept the faith. In the future, there is reserved for me the crown of righteousness, which the Lord, the righteous Judge, will give me on that day, and not only to me, but to all those who have loved His appearing.

—2 Timothy 4:1–8

Like a great coach in the locker room, Paul calls his protégé to "showtime." He raises the stakes by reminding him that his solemn charge is before the Lord Himself. He specifically gives him a course of action, and tells him how urgent it is. He dispenses with lengthy explanations and instructions and says, "Just do it!" And he stresses the promise awaiting the one who is faithful to the charge. Paul recognized the call of God on Timothy's life and in love "asked for the order."

Eli, the Old Testament priest, did the same thing with young Samuel (1 Samuel 3:1–18). Three times, God called Samuel, and three times Samuel went to Eli, asking if he had called out to him in the night. Eli realized that it must be God calling Samuel, and gave the boy wise counsel. He told him to lie back down, and if he heard the voice again, to answer Him and say that he, Samuel, was listening. Without Eli's guidance, Samuel might have missed the call of God entirely.

Bob was another story. Nothing about his life or interests suggested he had any promise at all. He was invited by a woman at a local church to join a Sunday School class she had started. Because she targeted the class to boys growing up in poverty, a new suit of clothes was part of the deal. Bob attended the class

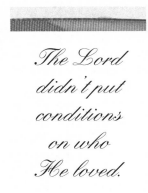

The Lord didn't put conditions on who He loved.

for a week or two, but did not return, so the teacher went looking for him. She found his clothes were already worn and dirty, and Bob didn't appear all that interested in returning. However, after a new suit of clothes, he came back. The cycle repeated. After a few weeks, Bob was nowhere to be found, and his suit had gone the way of the first one. The teacher was ready to give up, but her superintendent encouraged her to keep calling. "I believe there is still hope," he said. "Try him one more time." Sure enough, after that, Bob began to attend faithfully. It wasn't long until he became a Christian and eventually taught in that same Sunday School. Later Bob—Robert Morrison—left Scotland to become the first Protestant missionary to China. He pioneered efforts to translate the Bible into Chinese, and his influence was felt by millions of people.

The people you influence may not be called to vocational ministry or missions; just the same, they are called. Called to follow Jesus, share Jesus, and take action to serve Jesus. Like Samuel, Robert Morrison, Timothy, or me, they need somebody who will not only say, "You can do it," but also who will actually insist that they take action. This insistence makes a difference.

We were at an event for teenage girls called Blume. On the last night, near the end of the service, there was a commitment time. Many counselors, including me, were standing in front of the stage while the band played, and we prayed with many girls that night. My eye caught a young woman who was visibly upset as she came toward me. She was headed to me the entire way, and when she got to me she threw her arms around my neck and said she wanted me to pray for her. Pray I did, as she sobbed heavily. We were instructed to direct the girls to an area where counselors and leaders were waiting to pray again and to offer help.

I walked to the counseling area with Brittany, and she continued to sob. As we got near the entrance, she asked if we could sit outside and talk. She said she was afraid that no one would accept her if she told them what was going on. I told her we could sit by the front door. Another counselor stood nearby and Brittany began to talk and cry some more. She had come to this meeting to hurt herself because she felt like no one cared about her. She came from a troubled home; she felt like she was invisible there, at school, and even at church. She felt no one loved her as she was—that she always had to pretend to be someone she wasn't. We talked about how the Lord *did* love her as she was. But if we knew what she had done in the past, she said—many things that weren't pleasing to the Lord—we wouldn't love her and so she didn't see how the Lord would love her.

We talked about how the Lord didn't put conditions on who He loved—that He loved her, period, with all the faults and sins. She said she had given her heart to the Lord several years ago, and felt like she always failed Him. We talked about how His forgiveness was always available—that He sent His Son for her.

Slowly Brittany began to quiet down, and began to pray with us. She realized that we weren't going anywhere, weren't judging or criticizing her. She opened up, and we were able to offer her a plan of action for when she returned home. She trusted us that the support we were getting her was going to help her. She saw that we loved her as Jesus would love—not judging, not condemning, but offering encouragement, relationship, and real help.

The love we offered Brittany that night was more than passive acceptance, and far more than a conference statistic. Jesus called us to call her! To call out things in her she had come to doubt even existed. To call her to trust Him, to accept His acceptance of her, and to take action to change her life and her expectations. We're still talking and exchanging emails. She's doing better—learning to accept herself and knowing that Jesus loves her. Soon it will be her turn, when God's love comes calling through her to someone else. That's what love does; love calls.

For Reflection and Discussion

1. Think about and complete the following sentence: "Whether I believed them or not, people have always said that I would be a good _____." *or* "No matter how I may try to get away from it, I always seem to keep coming back to doing _____."

2. In 2 Timothy 1, Paul used words and messages of encouragement to call Timothy to faithfulness and courage. What example can you share of some of the most encouraging words someone has said to you?

3. Read 2 Timothy 2:2 and think of one of the roles you occupy today. How would you go about training someone to take your place?

4. Considering what God's Word says in 2 Timothy 3:10, who is *your* Paul, whose example you follow? Who may be following *your* example in the areas Paul mentioned?

5. Love calls. Is God showing you among the people in or around your life someone who has potential? How do you need to reach out to them, challenge them, motivate them, encourage them, or help mature them? What will you do today to get started?

Chapter 9

Love Heals

This morning I got up early and went to the river market to get some fresh fruit. I love going there—it reminds me of the market in Thailand. Often I see Oriental farmers there selling fruits and vegetables, and occasionally I get to visit with a Thai person. Today I didn't see anybody I recognized, so I went about looking for the vegetables and fruit I needed. I was watching the machine shell purple hull peas when an older man tapped my shoulder and said, "Do you remember me?"

I tried to think fast, but didn't recognize him. He reminded me that he had been a patient of mine—an evacuee from a New Orleans hurricane. Steven was one of the people who had been sent to Arkansas, and we had hosted him at our campsite, along with hundreds of other displaced families. I had been a nurse at the camp, helping a physician look after the needs of people there. Steven, skin-and-bones thin, had been very ill as he had waded through contaminated water to escape the flooding after the storm hit. The sores on his legs had looked horrible, and he had thought he was going to die.

We had washed his wounds and sores daily, and given him medicine. He had eaten good food daily and had been able to regain his strength. He had often cried while we cleaned his sores because he didn't think he was worthy to have someone else touch them. We told him about Jesus and how much he was loved. He also saw love in action from so many Arkansans who came to help. This went on for several months.

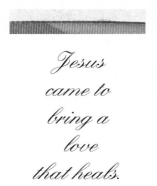

Jesus came to bring a love that heals.

The camp closed down, and with it the infirmary, as we were able to move families to more permanent solutions. I often thought about Steven, those sores, and how helpless and hopeless he had felt when he first came. I watched him return to health and as he listened to the good news of Jesus. But I never knew whether he came to know Christ.

That tap on the shoulder this morning gave me the rest of the story. Steven stayed in Little Rock and found work on a farm. He was at the farmers market selling vegetables he had helped to plant and grow. He was healthy and happy, living and working. Most of all, he had a glow about him—he *had* come to know Jesus! He had a huge, grateful smile on his face, and anybody could tell he was in love with life.

Nutrition and medicine can heal bodies, but we all have wounds that require much more than that. The reason I didn't recognize Steven at first was because he wasn't that same broken man who had been as emaciated in heart as he was in body! God's love had healed his heart.

The Healing Ministry of Jesus
In a prophetic look at the ministry of Jesus, the prophet Isaiah wrote these picturesque words:

> The Spirit of the Lord GOD is on Me,
> because the LORD has anointed Me
> to bring good news to the poor.
> He has sent Me to heal the brokenhearted,

to proclaim liberty to the captives,
and freedom to the prisoners;
to proclaim the year of the LORD's favor,
and the day of our God's vengeance;
to comfort all who mourn,
to provide for those who mourn in Zion;
to give them a crown of beauty instead of ashes,
festive oil instead of mourning,
and splendid clothes instead of despair.
And they will be called righteous trees,
planted by the LORD,
to glorify Him.
—Isaiah 61:1–3

Jesus Himself quoted this passage when He returned to His hometown synagogue in Nazareth. When He finished reading, as everyone was riveted on Him, He said, "Today as you listen, this Scripture has been fulfilled" (Luke 4:21). Jesus was saying that *He* was the one the Holy Spirit had anointed to heal the brokenhearted and preach deliverance to the captives. He was also saying that *they* were the ones who were poor, brokenhearted, and in bondage! The people who had seen Him grow up weren't ready for either message. Nevertheless, both truths remain: we live in a broken, hurting world, and Jesus came to bring a love that heals. Isaiah's prophecy that Jesus fulfilled presents healing love in four ways:

It binds up the broken, and heals their hearts.
It liberates the bound, and heals their will.
It reconciles the divided, and heals their relationships.
It comforts the mourning, and heals their grief.

We now have the ministry and mandate to take that love wherever people need God's healing.

Binding Up the Broken

Everywhere Jesus went, He found lives that needed healing. Some were brokenhearted over their sin, and some over their families. Some were brokenhearted over the way they'd been treated. Regardless of the cause, Jesus came in love to heal.

Brokenhearted comes from a compound Hebrew word. *Broken* means severed, crushed, or torn. *Heart* is the general word that

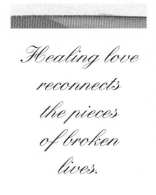

Healing love reconnects the pieces of broken lives.

could refer to the mind, will, emotions, or spirit. A brokenhearted person is one who has experienced a break in one of four areas—a paralyzed will, wounded emotions, a divided mind, or a spirit that is disconnected from the Lord.

How brokenhearted is the world we live in? Where do we start? With the 43 percent of US marriages that will end in divorce within 15 years of saying "till death do us part"? How about the 1 in 4 girls or 1 in 6 boys who are sexually abused before age 18? Or the 84 teenagers who commit suicide each day? How about the 34 percent (24 *million*) of US children who will go to bed tonight in a home without their biological father (that number jumps to an astounding 70 percent of children in many inner-city neighborhoods)? What about the 171 people who died from hunger somewhere in the world *since you started reading this chapter*? Or the 15 million orphans in the world whose parents have died of AIDS? Or the 4.5 *billion* people who do not know Christ?

Before we go further, we should stop and ask ourselves: Do I *really believe* that Jesus loves all these people? Do I *really believe* He can bring healing and hope to them? And do I *really believe* He can use me to make a difference? This is a healing partnership that God is sending each one of us to in our own unique ways. God heals in the sense that He is the source of all healing power. We heal in the sense that we are sent by the Healer, *and the healing only takes place as we go.*

According to *The Brown-Driver-Briggs Hebrew and English Lexicon,* one of the Hebrew words for heal, *chabosh,* means to bind or tie up. That's what healing love does. Like a doctor who sets and casts a broken bone, healing love reconnects the pieces of broken lives so unity and healing can take place. It dresses the wound, or wraps the injury until the broken area is working again. This can't be done by remote control. It takes a hands-on approach and personal care. A doctor would never look at someone else's x-ray to set your broken arm. He would examine *your* broken place and determine the best course of treatment.

Does this require ability? Sometimes. More often than not, however, it simply requires *availability*. Sometimes, when the need seems overwhelming, it's easy to retreat back into our comfort zones and surrender to futility. Rick Warren addresses that feeling in light of the global AIDS crisis:

> There is a sleeping giant—called the Church—that, if awakened, could solve this problem. Honestly, I don't think it matters what plan you and your congregation employ to become involved in solving this worldwide crisis. The problem is so huge that we probably need a thousand plans. But let's stop discussing it, and let's start doing something about it. We must be DOERS of the Word, not discussers of it. These times require action! And the bottom line is this: Are we going to love people the way Jesus does? . . .
>
> What is going to mobilize the church to address the AIDS epidemic? Not statistics. I'll tell you what will: When people really understand how much Jesus loves people with AIDS! How much does Jesus love people who have AIDS? Just look at the cross! With arms outstretched and nail-pierced hands, Jesus says, "This much! This is how much I love people who have AIDS!"

Which one of us, if faced with a life-threatening injury or illness of one of our children, wouldn't rush toward that child with everything at our disposal and risk our own health and life to bring that child to safety and healing? If we didn't know what to do, we'd get them to somebody who did! But we wouldn't rest until the "broken pieces were reconnected." Jesus calls us to that same kind of love for those He wants to be *His* children.

Liberating the Bound

"Do you want to be healed?" That's the question Jesus asked of a man who'd made his permanent home by the pool of Bethesda for 38 years. At first blush, it sounds like a ridiculous question. But maybe there is more than meets the eye.

After this, a Jewish festival took place, and Jesus went up to Jerusalem. By the Sheep Gate in Jerusalem there is a pool, called Bethesda in Hebrew, which has five colonnades. Within these lay a multitude of the sick—blind, lame, and paralyzed—waiting for the moving of the water, because an angel would go down into the pool from time to time and stir up the water. Then the first one who got in after the water was stirred up recovered from whatever ailment he had.

One man was there who had been sick for 38 years. When Jesus saw him lying there and knew he had already been there a long time, He said to him, "Do you want to get well?"

"Sir," the sick man answered, "I don't have a man to put me into the pool when the water is stirred up, but while I'm coming, someone goes down ahead of me."

"Get up," Jesus told him, "pick up your bedroll and walk!"
—John 5:1–8

This man was trapped in a no-win situation. To abandon the pool was to abandon hope. But to lay poolside, waiting for the angel to stir the water in hopes that he—a man who couldn't walk—would be the first in the water? That was an exercise in futility. Then Jesus appeared on the scene with a compassionate, yet convicting question: "Do you want to be healed?" In the original language, this is much more penetrating than it appears. Jesus was asking, "Do you *will* to be healed? Do you *choose* to be healed? Are you actively *committed* to the process of your own healing?" It was a question of the man's commitment to becoming whole.

Honestly, maybe this man really didn't want the life change that came with healing. He might have preferred sympathy. Many people do. Like this man, they have been victims of life circumstances. Maybe the sympathy and support they have received has so intoxicated them that they're unsure how to live without needing it.

He may have wanted attention instead of strength. Healing for this man meant returning to an everyday life of work, activity, and blending in. While that would certainly be preferable in the long run, some people are bound to attention-seeking behavior.

He may have preferred excuses to usefulness. As long as he lay there, he had a completely legitimate excuse for not doing much of anything, except waiting on the angel. Maybe Jesus's question wasn't so ridiculous after all, because usefulness suggests responsibility and accountability.

The biggest problem many people face is a bondage of the mind or will.

There is a type of healing that leads to freedom, but demands personal accountability for the choices we make. This involves trusting one's entire will and future to Jesus, allowing Him to heal from the inside out. While there are consequences and pain associated with addictions, compulsions, and other types of bondage, people sometimes would rather remain in their prison than accept the freedom Christ offers. They don't want healing; they do want to quit hurting, or for the symptoms to go away. Those who offer healing in Jesus's name must recognize the need for personal responsibility, but must offer His healing nonetheless.

It is interesting to see the man's response to Jesus's question. He didn't say yes or no. Instead, he started excusing himself by blaming the problem on others. "I don't have a man to put me into the pool," he said.

Jesus answered with an order. "Get up," He said, to a man who couldn't walk. Had He gone from insensitive to cruel? Of course not. Jesus met him at his point of weakness with His supernatural power. But He insisted that the lame man *own* his healing. And what a change! For 38 years the bed had carried the man. Now the man was carrying the bed.

Sometimes healing love must discern the difference between "fixing" someone and allowing God to truly heal them. Like the man at Bethesda, the biggest problem many people face is a bondage of the mind or will. Genuine love must be tender enough to help sooth their pain, but tough enough to encourage personal responsibility.

Reconciling the Divided

Christ's healing extends to broken relationships as well. Ever since Adam and Eve sinned, the human race has been separated from God. And ever since Cain killed Abel, we have lived with divided households, relationships, and with races. Jesus's death and resurrection have made it possible for us to be reconciled to God, and to bring healing to other relationships as well. Paul said to the Galatians that "as many of you as have been baptized into Christ have put on Christ. There is no Jew or Greek, slave or free, male or female; for you are all one in Christ Jesus" (Galatians 3:27–28).

Now we have the opportunity to offer Christ's reconciling love to people with broken relationships. Paul says that God has "reconciled us to Himself through Christ and gave us the ministry of reconciliation" (2 Corinthians 5:18). Certainly that means reconciliation between unbelievers and the Lord. Can it not also speak of being the peacemaker Jesus said would be "called sons of God" (Matthew 5:9)?

I grew up in a culture where communication was much more than knowing the right words to say. My Thai friends were soft-spoken in all conversations; being loud was considered extremely rude. And you greeted everyone with a *wai*. This traditional Thai greeting and sign of respect is done by placing the palms of the hands together, with fingertips in front of the nose and elbows down. And everyone participates. If a person is older and due more respect, then you bow lower and hold the bow longer. In a sense, it's a way of humbling yourself before another.

That's a good lesson for all of us. Proverbs 13:10 says that "arrogance leads to nothing but strife." So many divided relationships can be healed when we learn to model humility— something that often runs counter to culture, even at times in the church. Of course, it's not as important to bow in a greeting as it is to have an attitude of kindness, tenderheartedness, and forgiveness (Ephesians 4:32)—and to model that to others as well. To live humbly means to be willing to give up control of our lives, and to recognize our dependence on God first, then others. We can model Christ's love by showing even "the least of these" that they matter and are important to Him.

As with other expressions of healing love, availability matters most. April Fogle's rainy-day experience illustrates that beautifully. April volunteers with the Department of Juvenile Justice (DJJ) in South Carolina, where she leads two organizations of young women that meet "behind the fence." On this particular day, April had obtained permission to lead the girls on a prayerwalk around the property. She was looking forward to the fellowship they would experience, praying for the staff and youth behind the fence. But the Lord apparently had other plans! It rained the entire day.

After they finished their snacks, with discontentment in her voice, April told the girls about the prayerwalk plan. Due to the rain, she said, they would simply sit at the table and "pretend" to be at each prayer destination. Someone suggested they stand in the room facing the prayer destination.

"Sounds good to me," April said.

The first planned stop had been the Operations Room, where the girls first come to be "processed" as they enter the DJJ. Their meeting room actually adjoins the Operations Room, so as they stood by the door to the open room, April asked for five volunteers to read Scripture. Diamond was one of the volunteers who read Romans 13:1–5. After they read the verses, April asked who would pray for the staff in the Operations Room and the young women who would enter. Diamond raised her hand.

"OK, let's pray," April said. Diamond had other ideas.

"Miss April, does this mean if I am disrespectful to the guards here, I am disrespecting God?"

"Yes, Diamond," April replied. "That is exactly what God's Word is saying."

"But Miss April, Miss April" (you could hear the urgency in her voice), "it's saying that if I disrespect the guards, I'm disrespecting God?"

April assured her once again that this is what God was telling her.

Diamond immediately walked over to the guard and asked for forgiveness as the rest of the room stood in stunned silence. Tears filled April's eyes. April knew that God had changed a life that very moment, and allowed her the privilege to witness it. Diamond's attitude has remained dramatically changed and everyone notices it. How many more relationships will be healed? How much more of a ripple effect will this create because one person was willing to humble herself, and another was willing to be a catalyst for God's reconciling love?

Comforting the Mourning

A love that comforts the mourning begins with the sober acknowledgement that something didn't turn out well. Thank God, His love isn't reserved only for the land of happy endings!

My friend's father had been ill for weeks. The family had been at his bedside both day and night. We had been preparing meals for them, taking care of household responsibilities, and trying to be helpful. After a hard fight, the father died. He was a believer, so we knew that he was healed ultimately. While the family gathered at their home to plan the funeral, I was surprised to hear comments like these from those who had helped before the death:

"I did my part before he died, so I won't need to go over there now."

"I wouldn't know what to say if I went over there. I would just be in the way."

"They don't need me at this time."

Several of us went to check on them anyway, and the family *did* need someone to be there with them. They didn't need words; they needed our presence. They needed a touch, a hug, a hand to hold, a shoulder to cry on. What mattered most was simply being there. It's easy to find an array of excuses as to why we can't do something that intimidates us when it's the perfect time to be a reflection of His heart! Something as simple as being there for someone as a reassuring presence can mean so much more.

Sara, a former co-worker, called me one day and asked me to pray. A doctor had called her back in after a routine mammogram. She was terrified about going and needed to talk about it. We talked and prayed over the phone as she drove there, and by the time she arrived, she was calmer. I knew she didn't need to be there alone, so I drove to her doctor's office. When I got there, I saw her sitting on a couch, looking scared and lonely. She saw me and clung to me the entire time we were there.

We went back to the exam room and waited for what seemed an eternity. Finally, the doctor came in with a grim-looking face. While I listened to his words, I looked at the sheer terror on my friend's face. She had metastatic breast cancer at the age of 27. As he told her what he would need to do, my mind wondered how on earth she could get through this. Over the next weeks and months, we spent hours in the Word, trying to learn what God had to say through His Word and these circumstances. We prayed for courage, and one day we started praying for healing. Sara lay flat on the floor, praying that she would use her life for Him each minute of the day—even if it meant only a few weeks or years.

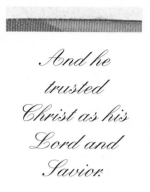

And he trusted Christ as his Lord and Savior.

After surgery, then intense chemotherapy and radiation, Sara hardly resembled the woman she used to look like. But in her eye, there was still a twinkle that said, "The Lord is using me to love others like me." She took every possible opportunity to tell of Jesus's love to caregivers and patients as well. Eighteen months later, Sara was still alive. The doctors didn't know how, but she knew why—Jesus! She was scheduled to go for her visit and tests to see how much the cancer had grown. While I waited in the waiting room, I heard a loud noise from the hall, like a celebration. I thought, "How insensitive to celebrate when my friend is dying of cancer." But in a few seconds, the nurse came out and asked me to come back, and I saw this skinny, bony body trying to dance in the hall. Tests had come back, and there was no cancer anywhere! The doctors couldn't believe it! Sara simply smiled at me and said, "I'm not surprised. Jesus has cured me, so that I can help others."

Paul talks of a comfort the Lord gives that enables us to comfort those who are in any kind of affliction, through the comfort we ourselves receive from God (2 Corinthians 1:3–5). Sara lived that, and the Lord let me be a part of it. She rallied for two years, then the cancer came back. This time it overwhelmed her weakened body and she went to see her Lord—this time healed for good. But not before she had fulfilled her promise that she would use every day of her life as a testimony to the love of Jesus. There are more testimonies to His love.

Khun Pim was riding in the back of a bus on a dusty road in Thailand. The bus stopped to pick up a passenger, and a big truck plowed into the back of it—right where Pim was sitting. He sustained the most serious injuries of any patient my dad treated who still survived. He had a fractured pelvis, a ruptured urinary bladder, a ruptured colon, and a fracture of his right femur. He arrived at the hospital in Bangkla in very critical condition.

Pim was taken to the operating room for a long, life-saving surgical procedure. He stayed in the hospital for four months before he was well enough to go home. While he continued to heal physically, the doctors and missionaries shared the gospel with him, and he trusted Christ as his Lord and Savior. After he went home, Daddy and others began going out to his village once a month for a mobile medical clinic.

Several years later, Pim's oldest son developed cerebral malaria. He was in the hospital for over a week, and in spite of every effort, he died. Pim went out and sat down on the breezeway between the inpatient area and the operating room and sobbed. All Daddy could do was sit down beside him, put his arm around him and his hand on his shoulder, and tell him how sorry he was.

Pim would not be reconciled. "How can I believe in a God that would not save my boy?" he asked with a broken heart.

Had Daddy been "just a doctor," he might have moved on to his next patient and left Pim to his own support network. But Daddy was a Christian first, and never stopped pursuing, praying, and visiting Pim and his family. Even years after he came back to the States, whenever he would return to Thailand, he would check on Pim. On one visit, Pim told him, "Every time an airplane comes over, I wish it was you coming back to Thailand to see me."

That's love that heals.

For Reflection and Discussion

1. Describe your most dramatic visit to the doctor. Were you or someone you know sick? Injured? How did it turn out?

2. Do I *really believe* that Jesus loves all these people? Do I *really believe* He can bring healing and hope to them? And do I *really believe* He can use me to make a difference? These are critical and pertinent questions. What makes it *easy* for you to answer yes to these questions, and what makes it *difficult* or *challenging*?

3. "Sometimes healing love must discern the difference between 'fixing' someone and allowing God to truly heal them." What would you say is the difference?

4. Read 2 Corinthians 1:3–5. How does God comfort you in times of sorrow, and what can you learn from that about being a comfort to others?

5. Love heals by binding up the broken, liberating the bound, reconciling the divided, and comforting the mourning. Where do you see opportunities in your life right now to reach out in one of these areas?

Chapter 10

Love Proclaims

It was almost Christmastime in the United States. In Bangkla, however, December was simply another hot month in a Buddhist town. It was more than 100°F outside. The sun had set, but the humidity made it feel as though it were 120°F! Everything and everyone was in their respective places. It was almost time for the show to begin.

We, the missionary kids (MKs), had decided that we needed to tell everyone about the meaning of Christmas. Though our missionary families were able to celebrate Christmas in our homes, the Bangkla townspeople didn't know about Christmas or what it meant. We put out the word that we would be performing a play. We announced the day, the time, and the location. Word spread quickly, and before long we heard that most of the town would be there. We had practiced for weeks, and were going to telling the Nativity story.

Being, as we were, in the middle of a very rural area in the tropics, we had to improvise a bit. We had a Mary and a Joseph, and were going to use a real new MK baby as Baby Jesus. We had wise men and shepherds, but we didn't have camels. We *did* have a water buffalo, however, along with a couple of sheep, a dog, and

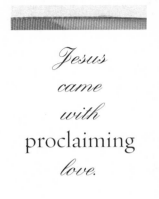

a horse. The play took place in a real stable, and we had made a manger for the baby. Even an MK, who was to be one of the angels, would hang from a pole placed across the top of the stable to sprinkle homemade glitter at the right time!

Jesus came with proclaiming *love.*

Everything in place, the townspeople came out to see what on earth this was about. Actors' costumes donned and adjusted, the play commenced. Our production lasted a good 45 minutes.

Except for the fact that the water buffalo didn't want to stay put, everything went well. As it came to a close, a little boy in the audience yelled out in Thai—"Do it again!"

What? Do it again?

Everyone started clapping, so we did it again!

When the play ended again, that small voice yelled, "Do it again!"

Again?

It had already been more than two hours, but we acted out the miraculous birth of the Savior one more time. When we got near the end of the third performance, an eerie quiet settled over the crowded audience. That young boy made his way through the crowd and laid his head right on the MK baby in the manger. Wrapping his arms around the manger, he cried, "I want to know this baby that came to the earth for me. I want to know the one that was born that night so long ago." And he started to weep at the manger. That night, 16 people received Christ.

Our play was a kid-level expression of a love that proclaims. We couldn't have articulated the finer points of the concept. We only wanted sincerely that our Thai friends would come to know and experience what Christmas could mean to them—if they knew Jesus.

Jesus came with *proclaiming* love. Matthew 9:35 describes Him as going "to all the towns and villages, teaching in their synagogues, preaching the good news of the kingdom, and healing every disease and every sickness." That runs contrary to the instincts of many today. "Preaching to" people smacks to some of telling someone what's wrong with them, of being judgmental, unaccepting, or critical. Yet that wasn't at all Jesus' spirit. What He proclaimed—published—was good news! And good news was and is meant to be shared.

One of the most dramatic responses to Jesus's ministry took place on the far side of the Sea of Galilee. A local man from the region of the Gerasenes, who had been demon possessed for years, experienced deliverance from his torment at Jesus's command. The witnesses to this event ran off and reported it, and many people came out from the town to see what had happened. Terrified, they asked Jesus to go away. As Jesus boarded the boat in the sea, the delivered and restored man kept begging Jesus to let him come along. Jesus had other ideas: "Go back to your home, and tell all that God has done for you." Luke concludes the report by saying, "And off he went, proclaiming throughout the town all that Jesus had done for him" (Luke 8:39).

This man had experienced something that was life-changing for him and good news for others. It was natural for him to proclaim—to publish abroad the good news! In fact, it would have been selfish and cruel for him *not* to share what Jesus had done for him. Do you suppose that everybody he met agreed with him, was pleased with him, or invited him into their homes for more details? Of course not. But he still loved Jesus and others enough to share. Your experience may not seem as dramatic, but it is no less life-changing. And God will use your willingness to share in order to transform lives.

This transformed man was not alone. Luke makes it clear that others there had been eyewitnesses of his experience. They, too, were testifying to Jesus's transforming power. And that presents us with a very important truth. Nearly every New Testament account of proclaiming love is in the context of groups and togetherness. Every expression of the Great Commission was addressed to Christians as a group. Nearly every encounter that Jesus had was in the company of His disciples. Paul, as well, almost always described his ministry in the plural. New Testament proclamation has as its primary focus: *all* believers receive the context of fellowship and cooperation for expressing God's love to the world. In short, there are no Lone Rangers when it comes to loving the world to Christ. Whether it's a children's play or a global missionary enterprise, we are called to a corporate identity as a "city situated on a hill"; to a unity that in and of *itself* reveals the gospel; and to a partnership that multiplies our efforts' effectiveness.

Identity—Proclaiming the Gospel Through Demonstration

> "You are the light of the world. A city situated on a hill cannot be hidden. No one lights a lamp and puts it under a basket, but rather on a lampstand, and it gives light for all who are in the house. In the same way, let your light shine before men, so that they may see your good works and give glory to your Father in heaven."
> —Matthew 5:14–16

To this day, the sun and moon are the primary sources of light for the people living in the mountains of Thailand. Occasionally, however, Thai people use a homemade source of light—one that I remember quite well from my childhood. They would put kerosene and a little salt in an empty soft drink bottle and cap the bottle off with a dried corncob. Then they would turn the bottle over for a few minutes, allowing the corncob to soak up the kerosene and then, light the cob.

When we traversed Thailand's mountains on a moonless night, the corncob light was the most common light source. But there were some important things for everybody to remember. First, the torch had to be held high so all on the trail could see it. If the torch were held down low, only the person in front would be able to see the trail. The leader would hold the torch high and yell, "Can you see now?" Only when everyone could see would the journey begin. Second, the torch carrier would need to stop occasionally to get more kerosene to the dried cob. Otherwise, the cob would burn up and there would be no more light. Third, as would be true for us today, too, holding your arm up for long periods of time brings fatigue. It was amazing to see how a Thai could walk holding up the torch for very long periods of time. But after a while, even the strongest had to have a rest.

The bottle-lamp lessons clearly speak to us on a spiritual level. Christian believers function in the world as lights function in darkness. Just as my Thai friends had to hold up the light on the trail so that everyone on the journey could get from one place to another, believers have the responsibility of intentionally holding up Christ, the Light of the world, for all to see. Moreover, we need to refuel at times. Otherwise we will tend to burn out. That refueling takes place in the form of prayer and being refreshed by God's Word. We also need periods of rest, so that our strength may be renewed.

How do we hold up the light of Christ?

Like the light from the lamps, we function as a source of guidance to others. When you can't see your hand in front of your face because of darkness, you surely can't see the walking path. On a steep mountain, not seeing the path can mean falling to your death. People without Christ face a similar dilemma spiritually. Without Christ, people live in the total darkness of sin and Satan's lies. As long as people believe that living "a good life" will get them to heaven, Satan will keep them from finding the truth. As long as Muslims believe that praying five times a day, giving alms, and making the journey to Mecca are ways to heaven, they are kept from finding the true path. As long as Buddhists believe that living in peace is the pathway to heaven, they will never find the right path to heaven. All these are paths to eternal death. And many people cannot see the path to righteousness because they are living in darkness.

How do we hold up the light of Christ high enough that all can see? Every time we share our testimony we are holding up the light. Every time we help someone in need we are holding up the light. Every time we go on a missions trip we are holding up the light. Every time we cry with someone who is hurting we are holding up the light. Every time we pray with someone we are holding up the light. Every time we show the store checkout girl a smile and give a word of encouragement we are holding up the light of Christ. The secret is remembering to ask, "Can you see *now*?"

It was amazing to watch the Thai hold the torch up high for what seemed hours before growing tired. Sometimes on those trips, an injured person was carried in for medical care. No matter how tired the leader might get, the group could not afford to stop for a break. Instead of stopping, the person second in line would take the torch, move to the front of the line, and all would continue the journey. If the trip was long, the original leader would sometimes have to take the torch back, but not before ample rest time.

All of us get tired. It's a fact of life. Christ's city on a hill—His church—must learn to keep the light going by passing the torch. When you see someone holding up the light of Christ to the world around them, stand with them. Pray for them. Offer to help carry the light for a while. And let others help you. Passing the torch from one to another to another to another, we have endless energy, What about each one of us? What are we doing with our torch? What is each of us doing as lights to the world? And with whom are we traveling?

Unity: Proclaiming the Gospel Through Action

In chapter 6, we pondered a remarkable prayer that Jesus offered for us, His church. He prayed that God's people would "all be one, as You, Father, are in Me and I am in You. May they also be one in Us, *so the world may believe You sent Me*" (John 17:21; emphasis mine). Do we recognize that it's possible to be proclaimers without using words? Jesus reveals how to do this in those words. He suggests here that when the world sees God's people living in unity, unbelievers will come to believe the truth that the Father had sent Jesus.

Paul mentioned the same thing in his letter to the Philippians. He encouraged them:

> "Live your life in a manner worthy of the gospel of Christ. Then, whether I come and see you or am absent, I will hear about you that you are standing firm in one spirit, with one mind, working side by side for the faith of the gospel."
> —Philippians 1:27

When God's people have "one spirit, with one mind, working side by side for the faith of the gospel," we attract people to God's truth. As much as we know this, we find that this blessed unity can elude us. We also know why this is so.

One of Satan's most effective strategies is to divide God's people. Whether it is in a church, a family, a denomination, or the body at large, the witness of believers' unity becomes challenging in times of strife or division. However, the opposite is also true. When family members, church leaders, and even Christ followers who are strangers come together in unity, marvelous outcomes occur.

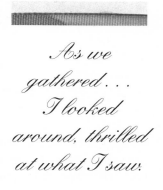

As we gathered . . . I looked around, thrilled at what I saw.

I know of a family that decided to team up and display a unified witness. Alan Moore, along with his wife and three children, felt God calling them to experience missions as a family. While the three children were home for the summer, the family went to Malaysia. It was hard work to put all that in place. Alan is the worship leader at a church in Conway, Arkansas. He had to make special arrangements to be away from his work for the summer, with no salary. They sold their farm, moving into a smaller home, and used the money left over to pay for the trip and provide the income needed for the summer. Would they do it again? Absolutely! The people of Malaysia, the Moore family, and the missionary they worked with will cherish that time forever. What an act of faith that was shown to those three children! They saw, firsthand, faith at work and the difference that working *together* made in people's lives.

I saw the same thing recently on a trip to Maple Ridge, Canada, at an event called FamilyFEST℠. The idea was to bring entire families together, along with friends, to serve and share God's love in different ways. As we gathered for our briefing, I looked around, thrilled at what I saw. Young children were there with parents, and a grandson joined his grandfather. A church leader was there with a group of teenagers, a single mom was present with her sons, and three generations—a grandmother, daughter, and granddaughter—also joined to serve. It was a godly, blessed gathering of intergenerational people who felt called by the Lord to minister together.

My friend Nelda and I could hardly wait to get to our own ministry site. Maple Ridge didn't look much different from the city where I live. We quickly learned that there were few Christians in this small town, and most had not heard the good news of Jesus Christ. That was one of our assignments for the week— just to hang out with the good people of Maple Ridge and look for opportunities to tell them about Jesus.

God uses the unity of believers to communicate the truth of Christ.

Nelda and I had a divine appointment there as we sat at Tim Horton's doughnut and coffee shop. An older woman asked if she could sit with me. She had been watching us all week as we ate doughnuts and drank coffee with those who came through the shop. She had been listening to us tell those we talked with about the love of the One who could change their lives forever. Each day, we had noticed her as she sat and drank coffee, looking sad and lost. As she sat down at my table, tears began to roll down her face and she put her face into her hands and simply wept. Then the questions came.

Why would someone want to help her? Why would someone care about her and about her needs? How was it that someone died for her sins? Through the tears, she told us about watching the children work alongside their parents this week. She said that they told her about Jesus and how much He loved her and that they loved her. She told us that she knew it was true because children *showed* her the love of Jesus. With the tears continuing, she asked Jesus into her heart and to be Lord of her life.

What a day! What power there is when people, even those in the same family, come together in love and unity to serve, care, and share. Speaker, teacher, author, and mom Kimberly Sowell discovered the same thing when she led a group from her church to St. Ann Parish, Trelawny, Jamaica, to help local churches conduct Vacation Bible Schools. They truly fell in love with the Jamaican people as they all enjoyed some satisfying moments of fellowship with the women in the churches.

> We had some sweet moments of fellowship with the ladies of the churches. We laughed together, cried together, sang praises to God together, prayed together, and studied the precious Word together—in unity. The children were so welcoming at the VBS as well, and we were blessed with many, many unchurched youth and children who came to know the Lord during VBS.

More than a human dynamic, unity produces a spiritual dynamic as well. Is it possible that the Holy Spirit works more freely and powerfully when God's people are together in unity? No doubt about it. Kimberly testified that as they shared the gospel on the streets, they met countless people of all ages whose hearts God had prepared for the gospel. People hunted them down asking for Bibles. They kept asking specific questions about the gospel.

> One thing I heard repeatedly as we witnessed to people in the streets: God had already been speaking to their hearts. God had been nudging them, making them aware of their sinfulness and their need for a Savior; showing them the truth about Jesus and impressing them to give their hearts to Jesus. God had us to show up at the right places at the appointed times for us to help those precious ones to take that final step into His family.

What comes first—the prepared heart of the unbeliever or the unified hearts of the believers? It's difficult to say. But one thing is true: God uses the unity of believers to communicate the truth of Christ profoundly to an open heart. Oh, and He also uses unity to reach an entirely new generation of servants. Kimberly shared with me recently that one of the volunteers who served on her team has made a full-time commitment to international missions.

Togetherness: Proclaiming the Gospel Through Multiplication
Snow is nonexistent in Thailand. If you have never seen it, it's hard to imagine what snow is like. How do you describe the feel,

look, smell—the sense of snow? How do you describe what it's like to walk in fresh powdery snow or crunchy, three-day-old snow? It is almost impossible! You can't fully comprehend snow until you have experienced it.

The same is true for the lost who try to imagine Christ. It is impossible without experiencing Him! You can't miss what you have never had. There are 4.5 billion lost people in the world who have not yet seen Christ to know that He's what is not only missing in their lives, but give them the reason for living. It would take 125 years for one person to say the name of Jesus to each of those 4.5 billion people, one at a time. Imagine what could happen if we joined forces! We could shorten that time by extreme measures. The more people we have proclaiming the message, the faster we can share the name of Jesus to that 4.5 billion.

Do you have a neighbor or an acquaintance who doesn't know Jesus? Have you ever considered that you may be able to reach them more effectively if you pray and work together with someone else? In chapter 6, I mentioned my Muslim neighbor. She and her husband came from Pakistan to the United States to practice medicine. I have a garden out in my backyard and when I am out there picking weeds, or checking on what is growing, the wife often comes outside. If I start taking to her, the husband comes out and I have to talk to him; he tells her what I am saying as though she can't hear. I started praying that she would be able to come out and talk with me without him. I even put a prayer bench in my garden so I could sit there, with hopes she would come outside while I was there. She did not.

My best friend suggested that my neighbor might come out if we sat outside together. We did for several days each week for about a month. Finally, she came out of the house to us. I kept thinking her husband would come out, too, but he didn't. We had the most wonderful talk with my neighbor.

There is power in reaching out together, living out God's love together, sharing the love of Christ together. What didn't work with one worked with two—together. And my friend Jana and I aren't finished! I truly believe the Lord gives us friends to walk this journey of life together. Jana also has a passion for helping with a food pantry that feeds the many hungry families we have around our church. She can't do it alone, but together with the founders and other volunteers, they make it happen. Now, every time the pantry is open, they are living His Word together for all to see. We were telling my Muslim neighbor about it, and she asked if she could come help us to pass out food. Oh my, what an opportunity to live the love of Christ before my neighbor!

We can do more together as we live for Jesus.

Togetherness in proclaiming Christ has another purpose as well: it helps us walk through the difficult seasons and remain faithful to the mission. My husband always says that we are *in* the storm, coming *out* of the storm, or getting ready *to go into* the storm. My best friend, who is also my cohort in missions, recently found out she has breast cancer. This really shook her. She called me to go with her to the doctor and to write down all he said. That way, she could concentrate on what he was saying and ask questions. She turned to me while the doctor was talking and said, "I think I can do this because I know the Lord is going before me, my husband is beside me, and I have a friend who will go with me. Together we can do this, and then get back to living together for the Lord." She got it. She understood that we can do more together as we live for Jesus.

Nearly 25 years after the Nativity play, and the little boy, I heard that there was going to be a play in Bangkla—a Nativity play. In fact, the play has become a custom to share with those around the stable, annually, the good news of Jesus. I happened to be in Thailand for the play! That night, it wasn't missionary kids who staged the performance; it was little Thai children from the church there in the town. The town's mayor introduced those putting on the play. What an honor to see him! He had been that little boy years earlier who had been so touched by the birth of Jesus during the first play. Not only had he given his life to Jesus, he had "lived his belief" since his decision. Also, he had not only become the mayor, but also was a member of the church, and continued to be a light for Jesus since that night he saw Baby Jesus come—lying in a manger. What an impact He is having on that town! What an impact that little group of MKs had. We had done something far more profound than we could ever have comprehended at the time.

We held up the torch.

Now he was passing it on.

That's love; it proclaims.

For Reflection and Discussion

1. Are you typically wired as a "groupie" or a "loner"? Do you prefer to get things done with and through others, or to be left alone to do things yourself? What do you see as the strengths and weaknesses of each approach?

2. How does Jesus say we function in the world according to Matthew 5:13–15? Who to you is a good example of someone effective at being salt and light in the world today?

3. What are the advantages of working together with others as a team, as reflected in Ecclesiastes 4:9–12?

4. In Philippians 2:1–11, how does Paul say believers can maintain a spirit of unity?

5. What are some ways you can partner with others in your realms of influence to proclaim the gospel to people who don't know Christ?

Chapter 11

Love Gives

There's nothing quite like a day at the airport. I spend a great deal of my time traveling from Little Rock to various US cities and these trips are usually quite an adventure. First, there is the check-in process. Self-check-in computers are supposed to be a big help, but it never seems to work out that way for me. For whatever reason, whenever a computer isn't working properly, the person behind the counter is nowhere to be found. Before long, I find myself in a crowd of other people with the same problem.

Once checked in, I make my way through security. I am so thankful that airports are seriously concerned about our safety. However, the process can create quite the chaos. Remove shoes, coat, belt (I'm waiting for them to say clothes), and any other metal object one might have. My problem is that I have a metal cage inside my back that isn't removable! It always seems to set off the alarm. And, of course, there is the whole laptop computer issue. Not to mention remembering to pack the right size of lotions, hand sanitizers, and all the rest. Once again, I can find myself in the midst of a large crowd.

At last, I make my way to the gate. Once I leave security, I want to declare with Paul that I have run the race and am keeping my eyes on the prize—boarding the airplane (although I don't think that's what Paul had in mind). But if you're flying certain airlines, as I do, you have one more crowd to face: line A, B, or C. If you've ever flown, for example, Southwest, you know that they don't have assigned seating. Twenty-four hours prior to your flight, you check in online and print your boarding pass. There you will be grouped in the order you secured the pass. If you're fortunate enough to be in group A, your line will be first to board the plane. Line B goes next and then the poor people in line C go last. They are the ones who get whatever seat is left over. As you can imagine, those are generally the ones who have to put their overhead luggage somewhere 15 rows away from where they are sitting, climb over ten people, and squeeze into the middle seat. Well, you get the idea.

It is the nature of real love to give.

I want to introduce you to four men who probably felt a bit like the poor folks in line C. They demonstrated a rare and bold kind of love demonstrated by lavish generosity. Let's back up a bit and start from the beginning of their day.

> When He entered Capernaum again after some days, it was reported that He was at home. So many people gathered together that there was no more room, not even in the doorway, and He was speaking the message to them. Then they came to Him bringing a paralytic, carried by four men. Since they were not able to bring him to Jesus because of the crowd, they removed the roof above where He was. And when they had broken through, they lowered the stretcher on which the paralytic was lying.
>
> Seeing their faith, Jesus told the paralytic, "Son, your sins are forgiven."
>
> But some of the scribes were sitting there, thinking to themselves: "Why does He speak like this? He's blaspheming! Who can forgive sins but God alone?"

Right away Jesus understood in His spirit that they were reasoning like this within themselves and said to them, "Why are you reasoning these things in your hearts? Which is easier: to say to the paralytic, 'Your sins are forgiven,' or to say, 'Get up, pick up your stretcher, and walk'? But so you may know that the Son of Man has authority on earth to forgive sins," He told the paralytic, "I tell you: get up, pick up your stretcher, and go home."

Immediately he got up, picked up the stretcher, and went out in front of everyone. As a result, they were all astounded and gave glory to God, saying, "We have never seen anything like this!"
—Mark 2:1–12

It is the nature of real love to give. When asked about eternal life, Jesus told Nicodemus that "God loved the world in this way: He gave" (John 3:16). When asked about loving neighbors as we love ourselves, Jesus told a story about a despised, hated Samaritan who helped a wounded Jew. The Samaritan loved him by giving to meet the need. In describing the ultimate expression of love, Jesus said, "No one has greater love than this, that someone would lay down his life for his friends" (John 15:13). What Jesus Himself modeled, He now encourages us to do. In ways that are sometimes simple and sometimes extravagant, sometimes practical and sometimes warm and fuzzy, love gives. The actions of these four extraordinary friends, as well as Jesus' story of the good Samaritan, serve as an excellent model of generous love.

Who were these four men? Where did they come from? How did they know the paralytic? Scripture is not very clear on all of that. Yet we do know that they were four who decided to work together to meet a paralyzed man's need and there is much we can learn from them. Yes, it was ultimately Christ who met the need, but what if they hadn't cared enough to give their time, money (somebody had to pay for that roof!), and attention? In taking action with love that gives, these men showed compassionate interest, acted on a plan until their task was complete, and confronted the challenges in front of them with faith and creativity.

Love Gives with Compassionate Interest

Have you ever heard the joke, "I'm so broke, I can't afford to pay attention"? Unfortunately, for many people that isn't a joke, but reality. But not for these men. They were interested enough in his problem to want to help him. Remember, there were no social services like welfare back then. This paralytic probably sat out on the streets, begging for money all day long. Without going into great detail, think about the sanitation ramifications of that. He most likely was very dirty, smelly, poor, and without much hope in his life. I would guess that, most of the time, passersby tossed a few coins his way without ever approaching him. However, four particular men noticed, and when they heard that Jesus was in town, they knew they needed a plan get this paralytic to Jesus and they knew there was no time to form a committee or task force; they had a narrow window of opportunity.

These four friends were willing to share, and that doesn't come naturally. As a mother of four, I can testify that at different times in each of my children's lives, sharing has not been on their list of top ten things to do. So, what did our friends have to share? They shared Christ. They knew they were limited in what *they* could do, but that Jesus could heal him. So they told the paralytic about Jesus. This can be a bold, sometimes scary thing to do. These men didn't have the evidence of Scripture to back them up, nor do we see that they had any personal experience at this point. What they had was a little understanding about Jesus, and a lot of interest in a man Jesus could heal.

The same idea is illustrated in the story of the good Samaritan. This story, told by Jesus in Luke 10:30–37, involves a man who, while traveling from Jerusalem to Jericho, was attacked, beaten, robbed, and left for dead. Along came a priest, then a Levite—two "religious professionals" of the day. Both saw the half-dead man and avoided him, passing by on the other side of the road. Jesus didn't address their motives because, in this case, *motives don't matter*!

In times of need, what matters most isn't theology, position, time, or other distractions. What matters is someone who will pay attention, first with the heart. That's what the Samaritan did. Jesus said he "went over to him" (Luke 10:34). He was open to interruption! He was interested. He was concerned. Are we?

Mamie knows how it feels to be on the receiving end of someone else's interest and concern. This single-parent grandmother is raising five grandchildren, working a part-time job, working on her life goals with the encouragement of her mentor, and growing in her relationship with the Lord through Bible study. Not that long ago, things were different. Mamie came to the Christian Women's Job Corps® (CWJC®) discouraged and feeling hopeless. Today she praises the Lord for what He is doing in her life and expresses great joy in studying God's Word as she seeks to know Him better.

One of our greatest obstacles to generous love is our busyness.

Not long ago, Mamie experienced a dream come true. She was presented with the keys to her own home. Working alongside volunteers with Habitat for Humanity, Mamie cut siding, hammered nails, and invested many hours of her own sweat and labor as she moved toward self-sufficiency. But it took people who cared enough to devote their attention to Mamie's need in order for her to make that incredible step forward. She believes God has brought this great blessing into her life because of His faithfulness as she has trusted Him and believed His Word. But did you notice that when God brings the blessing, He often does so through the concerned interest of others?

I am convinced that one of our greatest obstacles to generous love is our own busyness. Most of us don't get up in the morning looking and hoping for somebody to slight or ignore. Yet we can become so concerned with the details and stresses of our own lives that we're too distracted to "go over" to people to discover the need. We can, however, afford to pay attention.

Love Gives Through Decisive Action

On the first day of a recent weeklong children's mission day camp, each child received the gift of a New Testament. The children were told that they could do whatever they wanted with them: keep them or give them away—their choice. All week, the children heard mission stories, talked about loving and helping people, and discussed ways they could invite an unchurched friend to camp or tell them that Jesus loves them. On Friday, camp leaders asked each child what he or she had done with the New Testament. Without exception, every one had given his or her New Testament to someone else. One had given hers to a friend that had no Bible and didn't attend church. Another had given his to a neighbor. Yet another had given the New Testament to a teammate who did not go to church. It was a powerful lesson in how natural it can be to take action and give, in love.

"Somebody ought to do something about that." How many times have we had that thought, or heard someone make that kind of statement? How many times have we prescribed a solution for someone's need that some agency, institution, or other group of people needs to get up and do? What I appreciate about those young friends is that they didn't only talk about the problem, they carried out a plan. These children realized that all the talk about solutions and all their good intentions were useless without decisive action.

The good Samaritan illustrates the point as well. Jesus told the story to settle an argument. Everyone in His day knew that God required them to love their neighbor as themselves. So seeking to justify their prejudices and lack of concern for certain people, they would often argue over exactly *who* their neighbor was. After telling the story, Jesus asked the Bible expert, "Which of these three do you think proved to be a neighbor to the man who fell into the hands of the robbers?"

The law specialist replied, "The one who showed mercy to him."

"Then Jesus told him, 'Go and do the same.'"

Love that gives isn't limited by a lack of resources or money. It is only limited by a lack of willingness to take action—to actually apply solutions to problems. And this must go beyond the good idea or resolution stage. I always start my new year by making resolutions with the best of intentions. Unfortunately, making resolutions without acting on them does no good. As a nurse, it's not enough for me to know the problem. For example, recognizing that a fever can be handled with a medication is important but I have to *apply* the solution to the problem.

That's what the four friends in Capernaum did. They joined together and decided to take action. Let's think about this for a minute. They had to place this man on a cot and carry him however far to the house where Jesus was staying. I've carried people on stretchers and it's not easy, even for a short distance. Even a thin person can feel like a ton after a few hundred feet. So I can just hear those four men saying, "Man, you're heavy!" We don't know how far the distance was, but it was probably not very close. Had any one of the four decided, "I'm out of here," they never could have accomplished the task. The paralytic would have remained a paralytic. But they agreed they would carry him through the city to Christ together.

What's needed is decisive action.

First John 3:18 says, "Little children, we must not love in word or speech, but in deed and truth." So often it seems that we *talk* about loving like Jesus, but we don't. We let what others think get in the way of loving as Jesus loves. We need to act out of the love in our hearts, because of who we trust. If our hearts trust the Lord, then love in action should flow out of our hearts. What we believe will show up in how we act. If we know that the Lord loves us, then we will love others. The way we love the Lord will overflow into the lives of others. The Lord Jesus told the disciples that they would be known by the way they treated and loved others. The same is true about us, His followers today—others will know how much we love Him by our *actions*.

So what about the people the Lord has brought into our lives? How can we love them the way Jesus does? Responsive action is fine, but it puts the burden on someone else to tell us what they need—and some people have a difficult time admitting or articulating their needs. What's needed is *decisive* action. Not saying: "If there is anything I can do, just let me know." Rather, we can tell others, "I am going to do this today. When would be a good time?"

Love Gives by Confronting Challenges with Faith
These men undoubtedly had to carry their friend on a mat a very long distance, on a very hot day, on a dry dusty road, with no

bottled water or fast-food restaurants. In this entire passage, not once do we actually see these men complain or make excuses: "It's too hot. He's too heavy." They were committed to caring for this paralytic. We already know that if they had given up halfway through the journey, Jesus would not have been glorified, and the man wouldn't have been healed.

Our faith has to be genuine, and free from hidden motives.

In a similar way, the good Samaritan faced challenges as well. He stopped on a road frequented by violent thieves. He was one of a group of people that every "good" first-century Jew identified as worthy of hate. He obviously was going somewhere himself. No one would have criticized him for leaving the wounded Jew to die. Nevertheless, he faced the challenge with concern and compassion. He got involved in treating the victim's wounds personally, putting him on his own donkey for travel to a safe place to heal, and giving money out of his own pocket to take care of any expenses.

Meanwhile, back in Capernaum, when confronted with obstacles, our helpers in this passage were willing to adjust their plans. After carrying their friend all the way to Jesus, they were met with yet another problem. Have you ever noticed that helping others never seems to be convenient or easy? In this case, the crowd was so great they could not find a way to get into the house. These men didn't make excuses or give up. They didn't turn around and go back (my temptation on some days). They stood back, assessed the situation, and came up with plan B. We've heard of thinking outside the box. These men thought through the roof! Making a difference sometimes means making a hoist, carrying the load to the roof, digging a hole, and dropping through the hole. Outrageous? Yes. Expensive? Certainly to somebody. Risky? Absolutely. Yet this was no random reaction. Behind their actions was the steadfast faith that, once in the presence of Jesus, this man would walk home. There was no other hidden motive or agenda. There was simply authentic faith that Jesus was the answer.

At last, the four men had their paralytic friend on the roof (regardless of their friendship before this time, they must have been close friends by the time they got to the roof!). They lowered the paralytic into the house, where he found himself at Jesus's feet. What an awesome feeling that must have been! The four friends were possibly looking down at the scene in anxious anticipation of what would happen next. And that brings up an important point. We don't always *know* what will happen. All we can do is lay others at the feet of Jesus and let God be God. With pure hearts, we trust He is exactly who He says He is. That He is the authentic God, not a fake.

I'm reminded of a friend who can't grow a single plant in the most perfect of conditions. In an effort to keep ferns on her front porch, she was about to go broke. She would put the ferns in pots on either side of the door, and for a few weeks they looked great! Then something happened and they began to brown, dropping leaves like crazy until they were bare. To keep the porch looking nice, she repeatedly went to the store and bought two more ferns. One day, she decided she was spending way too much on live ferns, so she bought fake ferns. She was determined to have luscious-looking ferns on her front porch.

Just one problem with fake ferns—strong winds! In Arkansas, we happen to have frequent storms and tornadoes. Where do you think her ferns ended up when one of those Arkansas storms came along? Two blocks away in someone's front yard. Now the whole neighborhood knows her ferns aren't real.

When we decide to work together to bring people to Christ and to meet their needs, our motives ultimately *do* matter. Our faith has to be genuine, and free from hidden motives or agendas. Our compassion has to be strong enough to enable us to face obstacles creatively. Our determination to connect someone with a need with the Christ who can meet the need must be steadfast and enduring.

What obstacles do we have today? Maybe it is time. Or it might be family needs. For some of us it is health, and for others it is finances. Yet there is no obstacle so great we cannot overcome it when we work together with commitment, creativity, and faith. Imagine if only one of the four men had tried to take the paralytic to the roof. It would have been impossible. On our best and worst days, the best we can do is join together, do all that we can, and, in faith, leave the results to God. That is what our four friends did in this passage. Wow, what happened next! He got up, took his mat, and walked out in full view of them all. This amazed everyone and they praised God saying, "We have never seen anything like this!"

Jack saw the need and took action.

It is beyond my imagination the joy that had to be in that man's heart. His entire life he had been paralyzed, and now he could walk. Imagine also the joy in the hearts of the four who had worked together so hard to take him to the feet of Jesus. They must have been overwhelmed with emotions. Our friends took an interest, acted on their plan, faced a challenge, committed to the task, adjusted as necessary, and they made a difference in the life of a paralytic. First, they saw the problem, and second, they recognized the solution—Jesus—and they brought the two together. In short, they gave in love. Now, here's a contemporary example of a love that gives, in its ultimate expression.

Jack Logan, a dentist in Arkansas, was nearing retirement. Although he was experienced in volunteer missions, in recent years he had avoided missions trips because of the arthritis in his hands. The Holy Spirit kept working on Jack's heart until he accepted an opportunity to go to Mexico. On that trip, he discovered that he could, as others needed him to do, pull teeth—without any arthritic pain in his hands. He began reaching out to and treating hundreds of patients. It was as though he had been healed. In his excitement and enthusiasm, Jack began going on trip after trip that took him to China, Russia, Mexico, and Nicaragua. On that first trip to Nicaragua, he fell in love with the country and its people. He made room on his calendar for at least two trips a year to this country. He worked at learning to speak Spanish; and even though it was broken, he spoke it well enough to communicate the love he had for the people of this country.

On his last missions trip, Jack decided to stay an extra few days to enjoy the fellowship of other believers. He planned a fishing trip with a fellow US citizen, Bert Alexander, with a Nicaraguan pastor and his wife and their two teenaged sons acting as fishing guides. In the middle of the afternoon, as often happens there, a sudden storm arose, and the boat capsized. The pastor and his wife drowned immediately. Jack, Bert, and the Nicaraguan teens held on to an ice chest as a flotation device. As the hours passed, Jack felt himself becoming increasingly tired. The more of his weight he put on the ice chest, the less the others had to hold on to. He knew that in order for them to survive, he would have to let go. He took off his watch, gave it to one of the teens and asked that a message be given to his wife. After some moments of emotional tears, he let go and swam away from safety and drowned.

Jack saw the need and took action. He confronted challenges with faith, letting go of his earthly safety and holding on to eternal safety, his salvation in Christ. He went to a place of eternal life in order to give the others more time of life on earth. No doubt this affected the lives of the teens now and for eternity, and the results of Jack's sacrificial love will have deep impact on many for years to come.

"No one has greater love than this," Jesus said. But the reason Jack could offer up his death was because he had already laid down his life. He had given up his self-interest, overcome his own health obstacles, and taken action to serve others freely throughout the world. In offering himself at the feet of Jesus so that others could live, Jack was just finishing what he had long ago started.

He was giving; He was loving.

For Reflection and Discussion

1. Has anyone ever shocked you with a generous surprise gift? What was it, and how did it make you feel?

2. As we read in Luke 7:11–17, Jesus was in the midst of a great crowd, yet He took the time to give His compassionate attention to a widow. What lessons can we learn from this event about being aware of others' needs?

3. In Matthew 25:31–46, what kinds of decisive action does Jesus say He's looking for from His followers?

4. What sorts of challenges did Paul face in His ministry according to 2 Corinthians 11:21–33? How did he persevere through his difficulties to continue to serve and give to others?

5. What opportunities do you see in your life today to express love through giving time, money, energy, or care to someone else? How do you think the Lord is leading you to respond?

Chapter 12

Love Overcomes

In August 1983, Russell Stendal, a US bush pilot, landed his plane in a remote Colombian village. Gunfire exploded, and within minutes Russell was taken hostage, where he remained for 142 days. The guerrilla fighters explained that this was a kidnapping for ransom, and he would be held until payment had been made. Held at gunpoint deep in the jungle and with little else to occupy his time, Russell began to write. He told the story of his life and kept a record of his experience in the guerrilla camp. His "book" became a bridge to the men who held him captive.

He wrote a letter home, saying, "I am in danger only of losing my life; they are in danger of losing their souls."

Through kindness, Russell befriended his guards. One day the commander told him, "We can't kill you face-to-face; we like you. So we will have to kill you in your sleep." God enabled Russell to forgive, but for the next 10 days and nights he couldn't sleep. A submachine gun was repeatedly thrust in his face under his mosquito net, but the guards couldn't bring themselves to shoot.

On January 3, 1984, Russell was released. When he said good-bye, some of his captors actually wept, as revealed in Russell's book about his experience, *Rescue the Captors*.

A couple of years ago, an office supply chain launched a campaign called the Easy Button. Have you seen the commercials on TV? An office confronts a complicated or difficult issue, and someone will pop out the Easy Button. They hit the big red button, and the office supply chain comes to the rescue, with the tagline, "That was easy!" I was shopping for some printer ink and I saw that they actually made the big red button as a fun promotion, so I bought one.

And love has a gritty, determined side.

There's something in all of us that prefers the Easy Button. Wouldn't following Jesus be lovely if we had one? Wouldn't it be nice if all we had to do was push this button and out would flow compassion, availability, generosity, and forgiveness? If love were only a feeling, and sin a problem of the past; if people were always wired to do the right thing and never acted out of selfishness, pride, or greed, then maybe we could put love on cruise control. Unfortunately, as Russell discovered, we still live in a brutal, fallen world. Sin and failure abound. And love has a gritty, determined side. Loving as Jesus loves goes beyond calling, healing, proclaiming, and giving. Sometimes love must confront evil, overcome pain, and serve the unlovely. Love overcomes. Jesus did. By His grace, Russell did too. Now God calls us to overcoming love as well.

Love Confronts Evil

> "You have heard that it was said, 'Love your neighbor and hate your enemy.' But I tell you: Love your enemies and pray for those who persecute you, that you may be sons of your Father in heaven. He causes his sun to rise on the evil and the good, and sends rain on the righteous and the unrighteous. If you love those who love you, what reward

will you get? Are not even the tax collectors doing that? And if you greet only your brothers, what are you doing more than others? Do not even pagans do that? Be perfect, therefore, as your heavenly Father is perfect."
—Matthew 5:43–48 (NIV)

Wayne, a discouraged pastor, was talking to a friend about a devastating meeting in which he had just been a part. His church was becoming increasingly divided over a particular issue, and many of the people in the church had resorted to politicking and criticism. Wayne became more and more burdened. When he pleaded with some of them to protect the fellowship, their only reply was to insist they had a right to their own opinion, and they were going to exercise that right. Wayne was heartbroken, and asked his friend to pray for them. His friend replied, "I sure will! I'll pray they will get right with God!"

"No," Wayne insisted. "Pray that God would bless them." Discouraged and hurt as he was, he still loved them. He understood that love sometimes must confront evil, and that sometimes the evil can be as close as our own hearts.

The love that Jesus calls us to presents us with a dilemma. Our responsibility is to love our enemies as well as our friends. That isn't natural. How can we love someone that we are hurt by, afraid of, or resent? It's important to note that this was not intended for believers alone. Only as we allow Christ to express His love through us is such love possible. Moreover, Jesus Himself went on to explain that this kind of love is not a *feeling*, but an *action*. Parallel passages call us to bless those who curse us, do good to those who do evil to us, and to pray for those who persecute us. These are action words! As we put God's love into action, feelings take care of themselves.

God has called believers to confront the evil in the world, but never to check our love at the door when we do. Although God is holy, He never stops loving those who are not. When we love even those who don't love us, we reflect a desire to be like our heavenly Father. As the light consistently shines on everyone (good and evil), and the rain nourishes everyone (good and evil), we are to touch *everyone* with the precious love of Jesus, regardless of their behavior, No, this isn't natural—

it's supernatural. It's the Holy Spirit manifesting Christ's supernatural love, even to those who may not return love.

Sometimes, in an effort to stay away from that which we consider sinful, Christians face the temptation to avoid the very people Jesus died for us to reach! We must remember that Jesus came to overcome the sin that holds *everybody* captive. It was never His intention to isolate us from people who still need to be freed.

Throughout the kingdom, God is raising up believers to step outside the comfortable to love people in their own environment. Let's look at an example: the Gold Coin Ministry. Sandy Wisdom-Martin describes the opportunity she experienced to be involved in a ministry to exotic dancers in East St. Louis, Illinois.

It was way beyond my comfort zone, but I thought, Let's give it a try. We started collecting items to put in canvas bags for the dancers—items like Bibles, tracts, and lotions. Then the phone calls came. Phone calls about the ministry—what we were doing, what we weren't doing, what we were collecting, how we were witnessing, everything imaginable under the sun. I didn't know there were so many different things with one ministry people could be upset about.

On top of all the phone calls, we were told we were wasting our time because we would not get into one club. We were working with a Christian who does this ministry in San Antonio. So, we took a fruit basket in the club. Nothing could have prepared me for the things I saw. And the person, very easily, gained us entrance into the club. I promise you, I was stunned. We went back to the car to get gift bags.

When we returned to the club, the manager escorted us back to the dressing room where we could talk and visit with the girls. We were able to share Bibles and gift bags and gold dollar coins. We told the women they were more precious than gold to God. We told them God loved them and cared about them and had a plan for their lives. On my team, Sue, a former missionary, talked to a girl in a corner. The girl told her, "My mom's been trying to get me into church." I looked over and saw my friend Becky leaning over three naked girls praying with them.

And by the time we left, I was so overwhelmed by the experience and so overcome by emotion that I could barely make it out of the club. As I reflect, I think there were a lot of things going through my heart and mind, such as the lifestyle these beautiful young women were trapped in, the miracle of us getting inside the club, the opportunity to witness and pray with the girls, a recognition of God's work in this ministry, but also a profound sense of gratitude that God allowed me to have a part of this ministry. All that exploded in me in the parking lot of the Diamond Cabaret.

Sally gives piano lessons. Months before the ministry, one of her students asked for prayer. She said she wanted her mom to find a new job. Sally asked the girl, "What does your mom do?" And the girl said, "She is a dancer." So Sally began praying. On that ministry day, somehow God worked it out for Sally to go into a club. And who was the first person she should see? It was the child's mother, and she asked, "Sally, what are you doing in a place like this?" Sally said, "I'm here to tell you that God loves you and cares for you and has a plan for your life." And she was able to witness to that woman.

After teams went to strip clubs, they went out on the street to deliver bags and bottles of water, and tell people about Jesus. There were five professions of faith during the Gold Coin Ministry. Months later we were told a woman showed up at the Christian Activity Center in East St. Louis. This is a Baptist center that ministers to inner-city children and youth. Gail, the volunteer at the front desk, was with us at the Gold Coin Ministry. She said a woman came in the Christian Activity Center carrying an empty bottle of water that had the Gold Coin Ministry label and told the plan of salvation. That woman said to Gail, "I just want you to know that a few months ago some women came through this community giving out bags and bottles of water. I took the bottle and read the label. And since that time, I have accepted Christ and joined a church. And I just wanted to stop by and thank someone because that bottle of water changed my life."

Was it worth it? Yes, of course it was. It always is.

Love Overcomes Pain

We have an outreach program at our church that helps feed people who need this help. The food pantry is near a bus stop so that those who need a hand can get there by the bus. Some Tuesdays, we have more people than food, but usually there is enough.

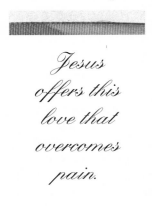

Jesus offers this love that overcomes pain.

My friend Jana goes faithfully each Tuesday to pray with the participants before they get their food. One day, she sat across the table from an older man and, as is her usual practice, she held out her hands to hold his hands as she prayed. She looked up startled because he had no hands—only knobs where his hands should be. Without blinking, she reached up and grabbed those knobs and began to pray. He started to cry; no one had ever reached up and held his knobs. This was more than an experience of physical pain—this man had felt awkward and unloved. Loving as Jesus does means sometimes reaching out to touch the pain that others carry.

Jesus offers this love that overcomes pain. He told His disciples, "I have told you these things so that in Me you may have peace. You will have suffering in this world. Be courageous! I have conquered the world" (John 16:33). The issue of tribulation or suffering is moot; Jesus said we *would* face pain. Yet He also made it clear that His followers occupy an overcoming position because of their relationship with Him. The most convincing proof of that victorious life, He said, is prevailing peace. This peace is based on our relationship with Him; it is in Him we have peace.

For believers, the power to overcome pain—ours and others'—is secured by the fact that Jesus has already overcome the world. If we can ever fully grasp that, this truth can change forever the way we approach seemingly impossible situations. When the Japanese bombed Pearl Harbor, and millions of Jews and others were sent to their deaths in the Holocaust, Jesus had already overcome that. When the Oklahoma City bombing and the terrorist attacks of September 11, 2001, took place, Jesus had already overcome those too. When hurricanes and monsoons have wiped out coastlines and whole communities, Jesus had overcome those catastrophes already. When the world has faced disasters, fears, pestilence, and destruction, it has done so from a position of the Lord Jesus having overcome. Neither the cataclysmic tragedies of our day nor the personal challenges we face as individuals will ever separate us from the love of Jesus Christ.

How can we look at tragedy and evil and say we can have peace because our Savior overcame the world? Because He died for the sin that prompted it all. Regardless of who causes the pain inflicted on others, the evil behind it is evil and the guilt of it that God's Son willingly, lovingly, bore. Jesus also loves those who perpetrate evil, and the people who experience pain because of it. Moreover, He redeems our lives from the destructiveness of it. He redeemed our lives from the pit. He brings healing, hope, and help to shattered worlds and broken hearts. And no evil is greater than His ability to bring peace and solace. Jesus also has limited evil's days. No matter how grave or severe, He has promised a day when all of this will be no more. One day, God will bring His ultimate redemptive purposes to pass, and this world will hand out trouble for the last time.

Most of all, Jesus walks with us through the worst of life. Nothing, Paul said, can "separate us from the love of God that is in Christ Jesus" (Romans 8:39). Nothing. We have peace because we have Him.

Ma Mary was a wonderful example of this love that overcomes pain. She was a "friend to the missionaries" in Liberia. As a tribal woman, she never learned to read or write, and had precious few material possessions. What Ma Mary had was a heart of gold and a love for Jesus reflected in everything she did and said. This little barefoot Bassa woman helped people all around her. She fed the village children and purchased school supplies for them. She cooked for children's camps and shared bananas and potato greens with the missionary families. Ma Mary always had a sparkle in her eye and a smile on her face. She would walk miles every day, through muddy roads and oppressive heat, to minister to someone in need. How could someone who had "nothing" do so much good for so many people? Ma Mary was filled to overflowing with God's love. Quietly and faithfully, regardless of the circumstances, Ma Mary's humble life always proclaimed the sweetness and peace of Jesus.

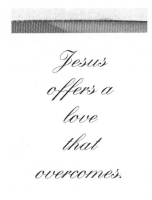

Jesus offers a love that overcomes.

Given the condition of the world, Jesus made a remarkable offer. "Come to Me, all of you who are weary and burdened, and I will give you rest. All of you, take up My yoke and learn from Me, because I am gentle and humble in heart, and you will find rest for yourselves" (Matthew 11:28–29). What a blessing to receive this gracious offer and to learn of His love.

I taught English to a Thai friend each day, and used the Bible as a textbook. He was leprous. Each afternoon I would go down to the clinic, and we would read from the Bible. The day he discovered he could have complete rest—in the Lord—was the day he gave his heart to Jesus. To that point, leprosy had given this young man no rest. He always hurt physically, and always ran to stay out of everyone's way. Rest to him was *huge*. He finally found rest when he discovered a new life in Christ.

Bishop Fulton Sheen also had a life-changing encounter with a person who had leprosy. While visiting a leprosy colony, he walked up to a man sitting on the ground, whose body was oozing puss from putrefied sores. As Bishop Sheen leaned over to talk to him, the chain of the crucifix he was wearing broke, and the crucifix fell into an open sore on the man's leg. His first response was to jump back, revolted by what had happened. But he said, "All of a sudden I was overwhelmed with compassion for this person. So I reached into the sore and took up the cross." Commenting on this, Rick Warren says, "I think that is the finest definition of Christianity I've ever heard: Reaching into the sores of life—where people are broken, hurting, dying, poor, hopeless—and taking up the cross."

Does your relationship with Jesus offer healing from pain? Is there a rest in your testimony for the weary? Regardless of the hurt, Jesus offers a love that overcomes through His amazing peace. Echoing the prayer of St. Francis of Assisi, each of us can ask the Lord to make us an instrument of His peace that overcomes the world.

Love Serves the Unlovely

Ahmed and Myriam are two Christ followers living in a large North African city, who grew up in strong Muslim homes. Myriam heard the gospel over the radio when she was 12 years old, and made the decision to give her heart and life to Christ. Myriam had never met a Christian and had never seen a Bible. She simply believed and received God's free gift of forgiveness and salvation through Jesus Christ.

Ahmed met Myriam when he was 18 and planning to go to Afghanistan to train as a fighter—to kill Christians. Through Myriam's testimony, God touched Ahmed's heart. Ahmed had a dream in which He saw four doors. Behind doors one, two, and three were worldly creatures and sinful actions, all trying to lure Ahmed to continue following the evil one. Behind door four was a man dressed in white, calling Ahmed to follow Him. Ahmed made the decision to follow this man, Jesus, who promised him peace and eternal life.

Today, Ahmed and Myriam are married, have two young sons, and are faithfully following Jesus Christ and sharing His love with Muslim neighbors all around them. Ahmed and Myriam want their own people to know the Truth. In the midst of almost-daily persecution, Ahmed and Myriam are showing others how God provides for His own, and how He always keeps His promises. They are true examples of how Jesus's love overcomes all obstacles.

Anybody can love those who love them, Jesus said. Overcoming love goes further. By loving those who position themselves as our enemies, we demonstrate through the Holy Spirit a love that "bears all things, believes all things, hopes all things, endures all things" (1 Corinthians 13:7). According to *Thayer's Greek-English Lexicon,* the word *bear* primarily means "to cover" (as a roof covers a house) or "to suppress." This word doesn't mean that love puts up with anything and gets shoved around because of a lack of dignity. Love, out of regard, respect, and honest concern for the real value of another person, will do everything it can to cover up and suppress the sin of that person. Jesus demonstrated a love that bore all things as He became our covering for sin; feeling its pain and enduring its agony in order to redeem the world. Now He calls us, through prayer, service, and forgiveness, to bear the unloveliness of others.

"Believing all things" means that instead of being suspicious and eager to denounce an offender, love believes the best. Loving persons never say things such as, "He probably got exactly what he deserved" or "He's so far gone now, he'll probably never change." God's kind of love expresses itself in trust, vision, and risk. If we're going to make a mistake, let us make the mistake of trusting too much. See others, not in terms of what they *appear* to be, but of what they *can* be. And even if it means risking rejection, disappointment, and isolation, love by believing the best about others.

What happens when we truly believe the best about people, and they betray our trust? What happens when we risk loving them, and lose? We see them in terms of who they *can* be, and they don't become that? When we lose *faith* in someone, we fall back on *hope*. Love hopes all things in the sense that it takes the long-range look. In the Bible, hope always refers to a confident expectation of something in the future. When we love someone, we refuse to take failure as final. Hope expresses confidence in God's power and faithfulness to change others.

Finally, love endures all things. According to *Thayer's Greek-English Lexicon*, the word for endures is a military word that means "staying positioned in a violent battle." The emphasis here is not on handling minor annoyances. This word refers to love that stands against incredible opposition, and still loves. A recent International Mission Board leader's report reflects this when he said that sometimes being a missionary means loving people who are hated in the eyes of the world. "Anything worth the blood of Jesus is worth our loving," he said. "We need to love the people who are the least lovable on the face of the earth." For example, there are more than 3 million Muslims in Moscow. Russian people often despise and look on Muslims as outcasts; yet, by 2050 Muslims are expected to constitute more than half the population of the Russian Federation. It is up to missionaries and local believers to reach them with the gospel. "And there is nobody trying to reach [Muslims in Moscow] with the gospel," the leader said. "Nobody! Not from our organization. Not from any other organization."

So where do we find missionaries to risk reaching out to people such as these Muslims and others? From somebody who will love by serving the unlovely. And that is the result of loving and being loved by Jesus Christ, seeing the need the way He sees the need, and calling, healing, proclaiming, and giving in His name. That comes as a result of loving them with His love, and enduring.

Such love is impossible, left to our own abilities.

When Jesus set His face toward Jerusalem and the Cross, people first cheered, and then jeered. Why did He keep walking to the Cross? Because He saw the need, and the need was greater than the pain. So He endured the pain to meet the need.

Jesus was mocked and nearly beaten to death by calloused, hard-hearted Roman soldiers. At any time, He could have called a halt to the whole thing. Why did He simply stand there and take the pain? He saw the need, and the need was greater than the pain. So He endured the pain to meet the need.

Jewish leaders taunted Him as He hung on the Cross. They dared Him to prove He was the Christ by coming off the Cross. He could have! He could have heralded His own deliverance at the hands of legions of angels. He didn't. Why? Because He saw the need, and the need was greater than the pain. So He endured the pain to meet the need.

There is nothing sentimental about this kind of love. It's tough. Determined. It is faithful to serve even those who least want it, much less deserve it. Such love is impossible, left to our own abilities. Yet through offering it up, and taking it in, by His grace, we can live it out.

Remember Russell Stendal? Following his captivity and release, certainly no one would criticize him for returning to the United States to find something else to do. Instead, he sought the Lord for direction. When he surrendered to God his desire to have another airplane, 23 years went by with no plane. God had another purpose. Russell started a radio station in eastern Colombia 8 years ago. Today he has two shortwave frequencies, three FM frequencies, and one AM frequency. His broadcasts cover all of Colombia and several surrounding South American countries with Christian programming. He and other Christian workers also spread the gospel through the written Word. Bibles are in great demand.

Recently, after 23 years, Russell received a new airplane from Voice of the Martyrs. Now he's flying again, air-dropping solar-powered radios, covering areas that are too dangerous to visit on the ground. Through it all, he's confronting evil, overcoming pain, and serving even those who would as soon see him die.

In Jesus's name, he's loving them.

And regardless of the apparent outcome, love wins.

For Reflection and Discussion

1. Complete the following sentence: "If there's one kind of person who gets on my nerves, it's _____."

2. According to God's Word in Matthew 21:12–17, how is it possible to confront evil, while at the same time showing love and concern for people?

3. Read Romans 8:26–39. How does the Lord show His love in ways that overcome challenges and pain?

4. In Luke 6:27–36, what are some specific ways Jesus says to love those who are difficult to love?

5. How have you experienced situations in which it was humanly impossible to love someone? How can you show God's overcoming love in these circumstances? What does it mean to you to "let Jesus love them through you"?

Afterword

The love Jesus calls us to is more than a concept or a set of instructions. It's a relationship that defines life and identity. It reveals God's heart to each of us by inviting us to embrace Him deeply and passionately as our first priority. That's why I said in the introduction that the most important character in this book is *you*. God's love is calling *you* to love the Lord *your* God. It's *your* heart, *your* mind, *your* soul, and *your* strength that will testify to the truth of the gospel for the universe around you. We will spend a lifetime seeking to understand the implications of loving God that fully. Isn't it a worthwhile pursuit, knowing that we are that loved by Him?

It takes time to "recalculate" our personal "GPS system," but I want to encourage you to begin. Imagine how our lives could revolutionize the world around us, simply by seeing through Jesus's love eyes! And the wonderful thing about serving a God of grace is that we don't have to figure out how to do it all perfectly the first time. We can simply begin! Praying with a listening heart. Reaching out with care and learning to discern His perspective as we do. Like a muscle in training, we will only get stronger as we are stretched and active.

We can love our neighbor as ourselves because Jesus loved our neighbor first. Think again of the ways He has proved His love for you, as well as the people in your life. Let's be imitators of Him. As we do, believe me, our neighbors will sit up and take notice.

So where do we go from here? I suggest we go back to the place we started—His calling for our lives. Remember, that calling is not primarily about a *what*, but about a *who*. We are called *to* love because we are called *by* Love. And Love has a name—a name above every name. His name is Jesus. And He's calling you and me!

Scripture Index

Leader Tips for Use with Small Groups

These ideas will support leaders who desire to encourage individuals reading *Called to Love* in a group, such as:

- reading and book-club sessions
- missions meetings or associational breakout times
- small-group Bible study
- other group of your choice

Praying About Your Goals

Agree in prayer about how God can make you and your group members more sensitive to what *Called to Love* expresses regarding God's call to compassionate thinking and behavior.

1. When will you gather? Weekly, monthly, or in a one-time event to discuss the book? Will you look at content chapter by chapter or as a whole? Where will you meet and at what time?
2. What will be your approach—casual conversation or more structured? For example:
   - Each of your reading group members might complete their reading independently, and then gather to discuss each person's impressions. Or, you might choose to discuss the book by section or by chapter.
   - Bible study groups might use the Scripture index to focus book discussion.
   - Your missions group might study the senses motifs that the author uses to show how we can answer God's call to receive His love and to love Him and others. Your group can examine what each chapter prompts in their minds as practical opportunities to live out God's call to love others in their communities and the world.
3. Decide your group context and the varied approaches you'll use.
4. Determine the format of your get-togethers. For example:
   - Play worship selections and allow for casual fellowship during the first 15 minutes of your gathering.
   - Then open with prayer and follow by reading a selected Scripture from the chapter(s) you'll discuss.
   - Plan to allow enough group time for each of your sessions.

Publicize Your Group

1. Send invitations by email, flyer, phone message, mailed invitation, and announcements in bulletins; or post online.
2. Recruit participants. Talk with friends, family, church, and association members to see who will benefit by attending the group experience.
3. Post online follow-up messages about your meetings and provide contact information for others who might want to participate. You or someone in your group can communicate by blogging or twittering.

Plan Your Group Time

1. Consider room decor or an interest center at your event; something that relates to the compassionate action theme delineated in *Called to Love*. (For example, see www.WorldCraftsVillage.com for relevant event ideas and plans to help the poor around the world through Fair Trade.)
2. Plan icebreakers that can be used at your first meeting—fun fellowship ideas that connect with *Called to Love* and its chapter content. For example:
   - Ask participants to draw outlines of their hands, cut them out, and create a poster together. Write the theme of the poster as Called to Love. Group members can complete this sentence, writing it on their paper hands: *I am called to share God's love by using my hands to help* _____. Glue or tape the hands onto the poster together and mount on a wall or easel to remain in view during meetings.
   - Tell a favorite memory about loving others as God calls us to love.
   - Name the most compassionate person each of them has ever known and tell why.
3. Serve snacks. Recruit a friend to help prepare. Appetizers and finger foods are better for parties than entrées. Food/refreshments (could center on a story told in the book, a country, or a location special to your group).
4. Select reflection questions from each chapter for use as discussion starters.
5. Consider how to bring the book discussion to a close. For example, wrap up your meeting—whether it be one or many times that you gather—by inviting each group member, who is comfortable with doing so, to say a sentence prayer sharing what the group time has meant personally.

Discover a world of hope

WorldCrafts℠, a Fair Trade Federation member, imports and offers you custom-made Called to Love items from artisans around the globe. Visit www.WorldCraftsVillage .com and see some 200 other handmade items. You'll see more about artisans and easy ways to share WorldCrafts with family and friends through mini parties or larger events. Order online or call us toll free: 1-800-968-7301.

Your purchases give artisans and their families hope for a better life.

www.WorldCraftsVillage.com
100 Missy Ridge Birmingham, Alabama 35242
WorldCrafts, a Fair Trade Federation member

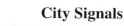
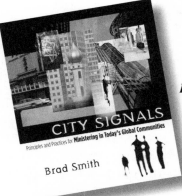